T0329439

People-Centred Public Works Programmes:

A Strategy for Poverty Alleviation and Rural Development in sub-Saharan Africa?

Costain Tandi & Munyaradzi Mawere

Langaa Research & Publishing CIG
Mankon, Bamenda

Publisher

Langaa RPCIG
Langaa Research & Publishing Common Initiative Group
P.O. Box 902 Mankon
Bamenda
North West Region
Cameroon
Langaagrp@gmail.com
www.langaa-rpcig.net

Distributed in and outside N. America by African Books Collective
orders@africanbookscollective.com
www.africanbookscollective.com

ISBN-10: 9956-550-48-5

ISBN-13: 978-9956-550-48-7

© Costain Tandi & Munyaradzi Mawere 2018

Authors' Biography

Costain Tandi is a Graduate teacher for Advanced level History and Sociology as well as Head of Department (Humanities) at Rufaro High School in Chatsworth, Zimbabwe. He holds a Master of Arts Degree in Development Studies from Midlands State University; Bachelor of Arts 4th year Honours Degree in History from Great Zimbabwe University; Bachelor of Arts General Degree from the University of Zimbabwe; Graduate Certificate in Education from Great Zimbabwe University; An Executive Certificate in Project and Program Monitoring and Evaluation from the University of Zimbabwe; and An Executive Certificate in Project Management from the University of Zimbabwe. Tandi has more than ten publications and his research interests include but not limited to Indigenous Knowledge Systems, Climate Change and Variability, Rural Poverty, Agriculture and Community Development.

Munyaradzi Mawere is a Professor in the Simon Muzenda School of Arts, Culture and Heritage Studies at Great Zimbabwe University in Zimbabwe. He holds a PhD in Social Anthropology; a Master of Arts Degree in Social Anthropology; a Master of Arts Degree in Philosophy; a Master of Arts Degree in Development Studies; and a BA (Hons) Degree in Philosophy. Before joining this university, Professor Mawere was a lecturer at the University of Zimbabwe and at Universidade Pedagogica, Mozambique, where he has also worked in different capacities as a senior lecturer, assistant research director, postgraduate coordinator, and professor. He is an author of more than 50 books and over 200 peer-reviewed academic publications with a focus on

Africa straddling the following areas: poverty and development, African philosophy, society and culture, democracy, politics of food production, humanitarianism and civil society organisations, urban anthropology, existential anthropology, cultural philosophy, environmental anthropology, society and politics, decoloniality and African studies. Some of his best selling books are: *Humans, Other Beings and the Environment: Harurwa (Edible stinkbugs) and Environmental Conservation in South-eastern Zimbabwe* (2015); *Theory, Knowledge, Development and Politics: What Role for the Academy in the Sustainability of Africa?* (2016); *Democracy, Good Governance and Development in Africa: A Search for Sustainable Democracy and Development,* (2015); *Culture, Indigenous Knowledge and Development in Africa: Reviving Interconnections for Sustainable Development* (2014); *Myths of Peace and Democracy? Towards Building Pillars of Hope, Unity and Transformation in Africa* (2016); *Harnessing Cultural Capital for Sustainability: A Pan Africanist Perspective* (2015); *Divining the Future of Africa: Healing the Wounds, Restoring Dignity and Fostering Development,* (2014); *African Cultures, Memory and Space: Living the Past Presence in Zimbabwean Heritage* (2014); *Violence, Politics and Conflict Management in Africa: Envisioning Transformation, Peace and Unity in the Twenty-First Century* (2016); *African Philosophy and Thought Systems: A Search for a Culture and Philosophy of Belonging* (2016); *Africa at the Crossroads: Theorising Fundamentalisms in the 21st Century* (2017); *Colonial Heritage, Memory and Sustainability in Africa: Challenges, Opportunities and Prospects* (2016); *Underdevelopment, Development and the Future of Africa* (2017), and *Theorising Development in Africa: Towards Building an African Framework of Development* (2017) and *Human Trafficking and Trauma in the Digital Era: The Ongoing Tragedy of the Trade in Refugees from Eritrea* (2017).

Table of Contents

Acronyms and Abbreviations

ESAP	Economic Structural Adjustment Programme
FAO	Food and Agriculture Organisation
GMB	Grain Marketing Board
GOZ	Government of Zimbabwe
IFAD	International Development Fund for International Development
ILO	International Labour Organisation
IMF	International Monetary Fund
IOP	Institute of Poverty.
M&E	Monitoring and Evaluation
MDGs	Millennium Development Goals
NGO	Non- Governmental Organisations
ODI	Overseas Development Institute
OVC	Orphans and Vulnerable Children
PWPs	Public Works Programmes
SDGs	Sustainable Development Goals
UNDP	United Nations Development Programme
USAID	United States Agents for International Development
VIDCOs	Village Development Committees
VUP	Vision 2020 Umurenge Programme
ZIMVAC	Zimbabwe Vulnerable Assessment Committee

viii

Chapter 1

Poverty in Rural Africa

"So long people in the rural areas of the world are not empowered, poverty will remain forever a perennial global problem" (Munyaradzi Mawere 2017).

Introduction

How to deliver durable solutions to poverty has been one of the most debated issues in the current development discourse. Most countries across the globe encounter a lot of challenges in rural social development as they try to fit themselves in the "global village" (McLuhan 1960). This is because, of all the areas of the world, the rural communities remain the least developed at least infrastructurally and in terms of empowerment of the population. The World Bank has revealed that most poor people in the world reside in rural areas and the situation will remain like that as long as there is a pro-urban bias in most nations' development strategies and their allocation of public investment funding (World Bank 2003). This concurs with IFAD (2011) which postulates that the largest segment of the world's poor are the 800 million poor women, children and men who live in rural communities. These are the subsistence farmers and herders, the fishers and migrant workers, the artisans and indigenous peoples whose daily struggles seldom capture world attention. With the realisation that majority of the vulnerable and poor are such communities as those mentioned above, one can argue that poverty is mostly a rural phenomenon and empowering rural people is an important initial step to reduce or completely eliminate poverty from the face of the earth. However, it is worth mentioning that rural people (as with minority groups) have little political clout to influence public investment in rural areas.

Although the world has been optimistic about rural poverty alleviation in the 2000-2015 Millennium Development Goals (MDGs), the World Bank has revealed using statistics captured nearly a decade after the launching of the MDGs that, more than 600 million people are still poverty stricken mostly in sub-Saharan Africa (World Bank, 2006). With such obtaining realities, one can argue that progress in poverty alleviation remains considerably slow.

In an effort to reduce poverty during the time in which MDGs were still a global programme, the Public Works Strategy, together with other interventions were adopted by numerous countries in the world. The Public Works Strategy was adopted mainly on the understanding that it allows partnership between the government and the people which makes policy implementation much easier. Sadly, despite the introduction of Public Works Programmes and other interventionist measures as poverty alleviation strategies in most African countries, poverty remains a major obstacle to development.

While the interventionist measures mentioned above seem to have magically transformed many parts of the world, this has been the opposite in sub-Saharan Africa. This observation has prompted SESRTCIC (2007) to claim, loud and clear, that sub-Saharan Africa is the only region in the world where the number of people living below the poverty datum line is increasing. Echoing the same sentiment, the Institute of Poverty (2010) has observed that poverty remains a major policy challenge in the sub-Saharan Africa. What causes such 'chronic' poverty however remains an enigma to be unearthed.

Duigman and Gann (1975), following iconic scholars like Walter Rodney, have argued that the current poverty trends in Africa were caused by the exploitation of African people during the period of colonialism. Similarly, Chinake (1977) focusing specifically on Zimbabwe, has argued that Zimbabwe's poverty situation can largely be attributed to the disintegration of traditional African society following the inception of colonialism. The colonial regime was ruthless in controlling African access to land and the means of production. This also resonates with Moyo *et al*'s (2014) argument that colonial policies promoted great inequalities and perpetuated poverty among blacks, leading to the liberation war and the attainment of independence in 1980. However, Rostow believes that poverty is a result of failure by the continent to follow the footsteps of Europe or what he called the modern path. Besides, there are some scholars who believe that poverty in Africa is a result of geographical location, laziness and culture. Although these theories have received much attention in scholarship, we strongly underline that colonialism and its subsequent concomitants like industrialisation and urbanisation, socially, economically and geographically marginalise Africans from their status quo, leading to poverty. Against this background, the present chapter conceptualises poverty, giving an overview of poverty, its origins, as well as theories that explains it in terms of causes, resilience and perpetuation in [sub-Saharan] Africa.

What poverty is and is not

Arguments over how poverty should be conceptualised, defined and measured go beyond semantics. The conceptualisation, definition, and measurement of poverty is very complex. This is because poverty, as with development, is multi-dimensional. It can be approached and understood from different perspectives. Chege (1995) states that, poverty is characterised by inadequate shelter, viz, improperly constructed, overcrowded and lacking in basic services such as water and sanitation as well as homelessness.

Interestingly, scholars like Alcock (2006) posits that there is no one correct, scientifically, agreed definition of poverty because poverty according to him is a political concept, and as a result becomes contested issue. This reverberates with Hartwell (1972) who argues that there is no universally acceptable or unambiguous definition of poverty and that the first three categories of scholars who tried to define poverty (historians, economists and sociologists) failed to come up with a common view. Scholars generally view poverty as an indicator of lack of access to resources and income opportunities.

Poverty also has a political aspect, as it relates to the allocation or distribution of resources, and reflects the impact of past and present policy choices. The ways in which politicians, citizens and experts use the concept of poverty have very divergent and diverse roots in social, political and philosophical discourses. Poverty discourse draws on complex and sometimes contradictory underlying assumptions about what people need or are supposed to attain in order to have a minimal standard of living. These discourses argue about the obligations to reduce poverty among the individuals in the

4

society, about the relation between having and lacking, ill-being and suffering, and also about social life and individual agency. These underlying discussions and narratives are not closely aligned, and this means that the concept of poverty as it exists in ordinary language has an inherent 'messiness' about it (World Bank, 1990).

As argued by Muzaale (1987), poverty is a multi-dimensional concept that denotes a universally undesirable human condition. It describes varying kinds and degrees of human deprivation in society. He describes poverty as more than just a physiological phenomenon denoting a lack of basic necessities like food, health, shelter and clothing, but also a state of deprivation and powerlessness, where the poor are exploited and denied participation in decision making in matters that intimately affect them. Nevertheless, scholars seem to agree that poverty is a complex, multifaceted and multi-dimensional phenomenon (Mawere, 2017a). Besides, poverty is not a static phenomenon; it changes over time, across nations and changes within individual economic groups and at various economic levels, where there would be differences in the perception of men and women. According to Sen (1999) and Mawere (2017a), poverty means lack of necessities important for a day to day living, for example, food and shelter as well as health facilities. Yet, owing to ubiquity in literature on poverty, the 1998 United Nations' definition of poverty, along with that of Sen and Mawere given above, will be used for the purposes of this book. The 1998 United Nations report defines poverty as:

> A denial of choices and opportunities, a violation of human dignity. It means lack of basic capacity to participate effectively in society. It means not having enough to feed and clothe a

family, not having a school or clinic to go to; not having the land on which to grow one's food or a job to earn one's living, not having access to credit. It means insecurity, powerlessness and exclusion of individuals, households and communities. It means susceptibility to violence, and it often implies living on marginal or fragile environments, without access to clean water or sanitation (p. 16).

The definitions discussed above point to the fact that poverty is a multidimensional phenomenon and as such can manifest itself in different forms and is measured in a variety of ways. One can easily note that poverty refers to a lack or deprivation of basic needs. It is simply a condition of lack whereby people do not have access to basic necessities of life. In this book, we interpret poverty as a state of being without means of getting necessary requirements needed for day to day usage. Poor people's lack of shelter, food, education and health deprivations keep them at bay from the kind of life that everyone values (Gaude and Waltz wick, 1992). Poverty can further be understood through general classification of different human conditions. In the section below, we look at these classifications.

General classifications of poverty

Due to its multi-dimensional nature, poverty has been variably classified. Two major classifications of poverty are worth mentioning. These are:

Absolute poverty
Poverty can be viewed as relative or absolute. The World Bank (2009a) defines absolute poverty as a set standard which

is consistent over time and between countries. An example of an absolute measurement would be the percentage of the population eating less food that is required to sustain the human body. This means that absolute poverty denotes a universal phenomenon that can be found in all societies all the time, such as, the level of income necessary to finance the basic requirements of human life. This means that, absolute poverty can be regarded as consistent over time across the globe. Muzaale (1987) notes that absolute poverty is severe human deprivation. He explains that people in absolute poverty suffer from chronic malnutrition and are chronically sick; they live in squalor; they are poorly clothed; they lack access to health care and educational facilities; they live short lives and many of them die in infancy and childhood. Rural poverty in Africa is largely covered by this definition. Phillip and Rayhan (2004) also refers to absolute poverty as living below what society terms acceptable conditions for human existence. He further explains that this can be measured by nutritional intake of 2 500 calories person/day or human development index.

Relative poverty

Relative poverty views poverty as socially defined and as dependent on social context. It is a measure of income inequality. Ravallion (2008) postulates that relative poverty is usually measured as the percentage of population with income less than some fixed proportion of median income. In its narrowest sense, relative poverty is conceptualised in relation to the national distribution of income/expenditure. However, parameters of a concept of relative poverty can range from the notion of making ends meet or satisfying a socially acceptable minimum standard of living, to living in a way which is customary or average for society, and beyond that to full participation in society. Each of these parameters precedes and informs the definition process. Relative poverty remains a challenge for every society, rich or poor, and rural Africa is not an exception. The challenge becomes more pronounced in the Global South where the acceptable living standard is officially pegged and anyone who falls short is considered poor. Relative poverty intensifies as the gap between the rich and the poor continues to widen. Besides these two classifications, poverty has also been typified. In the ensuing sections, we discuss some of the common types of poverty in detail.

Types of poverty

Scholars have come up with several types of poverty. These include inherited poverty, instant poverty, hidden/endemic poverty as well as overcrowding and terminal poverty. Inherited poverty is caused by most poor parents usually passing on their poverty to their children. According to Hatla (2010), inherited poverty forms part of the unending poverty cycle. This is the most common type of poverty in African communities. In addition to inherited poverty, there is instant as well as temporary poverty. Hatla (Ibid) observes that in many parts of the world, instant poverty is caused by sudden hazards and circumstances such as earthquakes, typhoons, drought, bankruptcy, war and refuge movements whereas temporary poverty is caused by some of the same hazards as create instant poverty, but lasting a shorter time; for instance, rains come at the end of drought, loans are obtained or war ceases. This type of poverty does not last forever.

Besides, there is new poverty, hidden poverty and endemic poverty. According to Feuerstein (1997), new poverty is caused by the manifestation of circumstances which may cause individuals or society to be poor. Examples are income/savings of workers and pensioners being eroded by high unemployment, inflation rates, or small cash-crop farmers being ruined by high input costs and low prices of agricultural products. Moreover, hidden poverty can be similar to relative poverty, in that people may have adequate food and shelter, but they lack other basic needs, such as sufficient heat in cold weather or access to health care, and do not report such needs. Also, deprivation of remote populations may be "hidden" (Foster, 1998). Additionally, endemic poverty is caused by low productivity and a poor resource base, it is reflected by low income, poor nutrition and health, and often affects. The last two types of poverty are overcrowding as well as terminal poverty. Overcrowding poverty is caused by a population being heavily concentrated into areas of high density. This is most common in rural areas. Terminal poverty means people who were born poor and are more likely also to die poor. These people are regarded as poor both at the beginning and the end of their lives (Feuerstein, 1997).

Rural poverty

There is need to distinguish 'rural poverty' from 'urban poverty' given that the former is often discussed in conjunction with the inequality which is prevalent between rural and urban areas. IFAD (2001) states that three quarters of the poor people in Africa live in the rural areas. Matunhu (2011) concurs with these sentiments when he postulates that poverty in Africa is predominantly a rural phenomenon. We concur with Matunhu but underline that this reality is so given that rural Africa remains the least developed, at least infrastructure-wise and in terms of human empowerment. Rural poverty, which persists in most African countries such as Zimbabwe, is evident in the difficulties experienced by many numerous poor people who reside in the rural areas to meet the day to day necessities of life, for instance, clean and reliable water as well as educational facilities and what to eat.

Poverty, for example in rural Zimbabwe, increased at a tremendous pace during the first half of the 1990s, owing to the failure of the Bretton Woods Institutions (the IMF and World Bank) policies imposed on Africa. Friedlander (2010) seems to suggest that the poor people admire what the rich people have and it is their utmost goal to attain equality. According to him, the rural poor require more land for agricultural farming, a good road network to ferry their agricultural products to nearby markets, water which is safe to drink and readily available and access to clinics and hospitals as well as educational centres for their kids and above all jobs.

This seems to be a major theoretical loophole inherent in PWPs. Community development projects are carried out and administered by the elite or over ambitious officials who often claim to know what the rural dwellers need. Johnson (2003:57) feels poverty cannot be generalised when he argues that "poverty is a multi–dimensional problem with its origins in both national and international arenas. It can be noted that up to the present day, there is no uniform remedy which is globally applicable". Following from the above, we note that the alleviation of poverty through an interventionist approach like PWPs can be instrumental in bringing the people back to poverty as it stresses the view that development should be influenced by external forces. We now focus on the main features of rural poverty.

Main features of rural poverty

Rural poverty has many features. Firstly, there are limited opportunities for the people. What this entails is that quite a number of people in the rural areas have limited opportunities to resources and employment and sometimes even freedom to choose. For instance, they have limited access to credit facilities, education and health. Owing to poverty, it is very difficult for rural dwellers to access say loans from banks, clean water from the tap, and medical services from the hospital. They can't access loan from the bank, for example, simply because they lack of collateral security. We underscore that limited opportunities may include little chances of being absorbed into industrial formal employment as well as chances to attain formal education. Rauch *et al* (2001) notes that chances to have a decent livelihood through employment and market production are sometimes non–existent or they are insufficient and unstable. He stresses that nowadays people in the rural areas remain in the vicious cycle of poverty due to the fact that they are unemployable and they do not have those skills that are required in the job market.

The second feature of rural poverty is inappropriate assets and capabilities. IFAD (2005) points out that despite a diversified range of knowledge and the copying strategies and mechanisms among the rural dwellers, their capacities to take advantage of limited opportunities remain underutilised. For instance, the people in rural Africa have an advantage of some perennial streams nearby. Nevertheless, because they do not possess the know-how to run irrigation schemes, that precious natural resource – water – is wasted and remain underutilised. This is what Rauch *et al* (2001) meant when they note that rural dwellers have at their disposal numerous livelihoods and a lot remain unexploited in order to earn a living. This owes much to lack of expertise/know-how and [advanced] technology.

Thirdly, institutional deficiencies is another important feature of rural poverty. Most rural dwellers have little access to services, information, and markets, which of late have turned to be basic necessities for securing a decent livelihood. Nyati (2012) stresses that, this applies to access to basics health services like hospitals and clinics, as well as up to date information about market centres for their field harvests. As a consequence of deficiencies in private and public service system, such services are not accessible to the majority of rural dwellers. This works against the rural people's capabilities to make effective use of their resources and to manage their natural resources in a sustainable manner and cope successfully with changes (Rauch *et al* 2001). This is aggravated by the fact that many rural areas in Africa are not covered by media. This is another way that has detached rural areas from the rest of the world. And it is one reasons why IFAD (2005) notes that chronic poverty is more prevalent in rural than in urban areas.

The fourth important feature of rural poverty is unbalanced power structures. Quite a number of rural dwellers have neither the purchasing power, nor political clout to articulate their necessities to gain access to the private and public service system or to succeed in the struggle for limited chances and resources (Nyati 2012). According to the IFAD (2005), poor people in the rural areas are in that condition owing to the fact that governing policies as well as laws and other regulations (or lack of them) define their opportunities. What is required is simply a change in policy. They often find it hectic to bear the organisational costs associated with empowerment (Rauch *et al* 2001). Owing to the unbalanced power structures, rural dwellers lack representation hence they miss quite a number of opportunities. It is a fact that some formulated policies may not be considered to the situation of the poor people who reside in the rural areas, hence they need to be changed.

Drawing on our findings from the field in rural Africa, we note that Rauch *et al* (Ibid) left another very important feature of rural poverty – unemployment. We, therefore, add that unemployment is another important feature of poverty, though most especially of urban poverty. The Economic Watch Magazine (2010) defines unemployment as a status in which an individual person does not have a job but is looking for one. Nevertheless, there is a broad definition of unemployment which regards it as a status where people are without jobs and have lost interest in searching for one.

Unemployment can be categorised in four distinct classes, namely cyclical employment, seasonal employment, frictional employment and structural unemployment. Cyclical unemployment is a form of unemployment which is consistent with trade cycles. It usually transpires in times of an economic boom, and during these times unemployment reduces. The reverse is equally true during periods of an economic recession. Besides, there is seasonal unemployment. This can be regarded as a form of unemployment which rises and fall with seasonal trades for instance hotel catering and the picking of fruits. In addition, there is frictional unemployment.

Frictional unemployment is a form of unemployment that can best explained as unemployment which occurs when one is between two jobs, where s/he has lost one job and is busy searching for another one. The last category of unemployment is structural unemployment. In simpler terms, structural unemployment can be explained as a form of unemployment which takes place owing to a change in the composition of some industries. It is crucial to take note of the fact that progress in technology may convert an industry which requires much labour to a capital intensive one. This reduces the need for much labour in the said industries. Guich and Rusticell (2010) argue that structural unemployment is the rate of unemployment which is consistent with the inflation.

Scholars like Jacobs and Slaus (2011) note that employment is a basic human right and above all a major essential function of any economic system, as it makes a crucial contribution towards the economic welfare of people. It can be further argued that unemployment is a function of quite a number of variables which include investment, money supply, as well as the debt of consumers. The duo further note that, changes in all these variables have a corresponding relationship with levels of employment rates where these relationships are predictable.

John Maynard (cited in Wray, 2009) opines that a significant number of people residing in capitalist countries must work for a wage as a primary source of employment and income. Nevertheless, Wray stresses that the inability to obtain a job lowers the income of people and thus their inability to spend money. Owing to this, the growth of an economy is affected. Howell (2001) concurs with these sentiments and further stipulates that poverty and limited access to jobs decreases the productivity of most vulnerable groups and again lowers their capacity to have meaningful investments.

To get rid of the negative results of unemployment, Wray (2009) emphasises that there is need to put unemployed labour to work in socially productive ways through government expenditure that would provide useful economic output which as a result, helps to alleviate market failures. According to Burger and Von Fintel (2009), in a mixed economic system, high unemployment is an issue of concern for the government and concerned stakeholders as well as labour market participants. This is because, lack of jobs precipitates high levels of poverty and inequality, which in turn impacts negatively on the socio-economic growth of a country.

The nexus between unemployment and poverty

Some studies on poverty recognise unemployment as the most important cause of poverty (Novak 1998; Wray 2009 and Howel 2001). It can be noted that households whose head is unemployed have a higher risk of suffering poverty. This is so because the only productive asset that the poor have at their disposal is their labour power. Novak (1998) stresses that while debates have been ongoing concerning the nexus between poverty and unemployment, there is need to reinforce the debates on the contribution of employment to poverty alleviation.

Besides, over half of the household defined as poor in Africa are headed by a person who does not have a job. Since household heads are likely to have dependants, there is therefore a high risk of poverty when the household head is unemployed for a longer period of time. Swanepoel and De Beer (2000) identify a complex relationship between poverty and unemployment. For these scholars, poverty can be both a cause and a result of unemployment.

Owing to lack of clarification of these concepts, the debate has also spilled into the issue of PWPs. It is generally argued that while numerous socio-economic and cultural factors prevent the poor people from joining the waged employment, PWPs by virtue of their strategies and modalities facilitate their entry. Many scholars indeed support the view that it is one of the objectives of PWPs to alleviate poverty through employment creation. According to Ganier (1992), PWPs are a means of creating high volumes of employment in the short term in a situation of unemployment and underemployment. Islam (2005) strongly believes in the power of PWPs in transforming the lives of the poor people in rural areas.

However, the debate is interesting. It unveils one of the major gaps in the theoretical dimension of PWPs. The study exposes pockets of intellectual vacuums that need to be urgently filled. If public works schemes in Africa in general and Zimbabwe in particular can enrich the people with short lived employment opportunities, do they also equip them with some technical skills that render them marketable on the job market after the life of PWPs. Equally prominent is the question of sustainability of projects after the life span of public works and whether there are measures to ensure that the people do not go back to poverty after public works. Let us focus on the causes of poverty in general.

Causes of poverty

People's views about poverty differ according to their backgrounds (Chinake 1997). In fact, the way those affected by poverty conceptualise poverty, its causes and solutions differs with how the outsiders like policy makers, development practitioners, politicians and others, understand poverty. Chinake (Ibid) notes that the problem of defining and fighting poverty is more of a political and technical problem than a rational activity. This resonates with Alcock (1993) who argues that politics and politicians are the major cause of poverty since they run the country and are therefore accountable for the problems within it. However, Mawere (2017b) argues that:

African poverty is a result of the legacies of the most regrettable and extremely unfortunate events of trans-Atlantic slave trade and colonialism, which today have transfigured themselves into what has come to be generally known as "neo-colonialism". In any case, it is difficult to fully understand and appreciate the present poverty condition of any given country (African countries included) without examining its past events – good or bad – that shaped the present condition the country in question finds itself in.

Meanwhile, Muzaale (1987) points out that the general consensus is that Global South rural poverty is increasing at a sporadic pace. According to him, this is taking place despite decades of rural development effort primarily because the development policies and strategies were based on poorly conceived causal factors. He further stresses that:

> The guiding models of these development efforts have tended to be single-factor explanations of a highly complex problem and have tended to ignore such important variables as the historical, social, national, and international contexts in which poverty and underdevelopment have thrived (p. 79).

Muzaale further argues that pre-colonial economies were characterised by autonomous, self-sufficient indigenous family economic units which operated independently from the pressures of the international economy and modern state economy. Although these pre-colonial economies were susceptible to natural disasters such as droughts and floods, local level mutual social support systems did provide a reliable safety-net, except in cases where whole communities were similarly affected. Muzaale (Ibid) claims that those pre-colonial rural economies were superior to modern economies in as far as meeting nutritional needs and ownership was concerned. The colonial era was characterised by extraction of natural resources and labour for use in the manufacturing industries of the metropolis at the expense of developing nations. This is the genesis of the underdevelopment of Africa (Amin 1972). Muzaale (1987) argues that the post-colonial African governments have not done much to alter the situation. Export of primary commodities still continues while lack of participation of the poor in development planning has worsened the poverty problem.

Besides, the above historic factors there are some other predominant causes of poverty that also need to be taken into considerations when dealing with poverty. Idriss *et al* (1992) further asserts that lack of infrastructure also hinders development and mobility. This includes insufficient roads, irrigation infrastructure (for instance, dams, pipes), poor communication and media outlets that hinder communication with established urban markets. This failure to access markets also contributes to high incidence of poverty. They are also of the view that lack of access to markets and credit also hinder productivity, thus resulting in low income. Muzaale (1987) also support the view that the rural poor have many production constraints which have not received attention from resource allocators especially the issue of credit.

Demographic factors also play a part in increasing poverty. According to Muzaale (Ibid) the rural areas are characterised by the aged and the young children (who do not produce and need to be fed) and other unemployables. This he says results in a high dependency ratio that can retard development and contribute to continued rural poverty. High population growth is another important demographic factor that causes poverty.

There is a correlation between high population growth rate and savings and investment. If the population grows at a faster rate than what a country produces then there will be more expenditure than savings. Population growth rate also has an impact on fixed family resources, like land. Over-population in rural areas often leads to migration to urban centres where the migrants might become worse off due to lack of coping mechanisms.

Additionally, there are what Muzaale (1987) terms 'precipitating factors to the poverty problem'. These are periodic shocks for the rural population such as drought, famines, floods, epidemics, animal and human diseases and civil strife. Because of these episodic shocks in the natural environment there is seasonal dimension to rural poverty. This analysis of the causes of rural poverty saves to show that the causes are varied and interlocked, thus, necessitating a multipronged approach. Treating one causal factor may not be a viable solution to poverty reduction.

Measurement of poverty

Poverty is dynamic and as such changes over time and between places, thus rendering it difficult to measure. Writing about the politics of measurement, Scott (1998) noted that there was no one best way of measuring poverty since poverty tended to differ according to the prevailing situation, geographic location and season. There is need to consider the relevant local concerns that give rise to the poverty question. Mawere (2017a) argues that poverty is normally measured using poverty indicators, which are both qualitative and quantitative. He further explains that:

To measure poverty in a country, we look at the poverty datum line. By poverty datum line (PDL), I mean a representation of the cost of a given standard of living that must be attained if a person is deemed not to be poor (Zimbabwe's Ministry of Finance and Economic Development 2014). One may however be poor in terms of food provision and not poor in terms of other provisions such as clothing and shelter, hence we also what we call food poverty datum line (FPDL), which represents the minimum consumption expenditure necessary to ensure that each household member can (if all expenditures were devoted to food) consume a minimum food basket representing 2 100 calories. This means that any individual (or household) whose total consumption expenditure does not exceed the poverty line is judged to be poor. In Zimbabwe, the national food poverty line (FPL) per person as at January 2014 stood at US$32. 00 as compared to US$31. 00 of December 2013. This means that the minimum needs basket cost per person in January 2014 was US$32. 00 as of January 2014. Currently, Zimbabwe's poverty datum line is pegged at US$500. 00 with percentage of the poor being 90 % while that of the rich stands at 10 % as compared to the 75 % (poor people) and 25 % (rich people) during the colonial period. What this means is that all people earning US$ 499. 00 and below are deemed poor but poverty levels remain varied as we have other people earning say US$ 150. 00, others earning US$ 250. 00, and so on. Also, the above entails that the level of poverty in Zimbabwe has increased by 15 % since the colonial period, making majority of the Zimbabweans poorer than they were during the colonial era (Mawere 2017a: 118).

However, it is of great significance to measure poverty because it enables development workers to know who is poor, how many people are poor and where they are located. Understanding the characteristics of poverty can also help policy makers think about the impact of economic growth policies and interventions. For example, with measures of poverty over time, policy makers can assess if poverty has increased or decreased, or whether general economic growth policies and interventions helped the poor. Poverty data can be used to inform economy wide policy reforms and to deduce how changes in relative prices affect the poor. Scholars do not seem to agree on the best way of measuring poverty. Foster (1984) advocates for the use of the head count poverty index given by the percentage of the population that live in the household with a consumption per capita less than the poverty line and the poverty gap index which reflects the depth of poverty by taking into account how far the average poor person's income is from the poverty line. We now discuss how Africa can overcome poverty.

Poverty eradication

Poverty is the most bewildering challenge in any developing country where, as indicated above, on average the majority of the population is considered poor. Despite the concerted effort of various governments and international bodies through a number of elaborate programmes and measures aimed at making poverty history, there is still a worrisome trend of poverty throughout the world. Meanwhile, most African countries have not been spared by the scourge of poverty both in urban and rural areas. Since independence, the governments have undertaken some poverty reduction initiatives with the aim of reducing, if not totally eradicating poverty; especially using interventionist approaches such as PWPs.

Most people believe that the solution to poverty is welfare relief. However, Muzaale, (1987) argues convincingly that instead of focusing on relief, policy makers should make serious efforts to know who the poor are, how many they are, their location, their distinguishing characteristics and the underlying causes of their state, and what can be done to assist them and how the poor themselves can participate in alleviating their status. Land reform is considered as one of the solutions to poverty. Idriss *et al* (1992), argue that improved access to land can alleviate poverty by providing households with more production land. Dercon (2009) and Ravallion (2007) in support of land reform base their argument on the China land redistribution case which is associated with reduction in rural poverty and increased agricultural growth.

Idriss *et al* (1992) posits that improving rural infrastructure, such as roads and irrigation systems, can reduce rural poverty by allowing rural dwellers to have greater communication with urban centres through improved transport links to the markets and social services thus combating social exclusion of the rural poor. This resonates with Janvry *et al* (2002) who argue that improved road networks and irrigation facilities stimulate productivity and access to markets thus leading to increase in household income. Idriss *et al* (1992) feels the same about irrigation equipment which if improved will result in greater agricultural productivity and ultimately an increase in food and income security.

Ahmed and Hossain (1990) using the case of Bangladesh also argue that an improvement in agriculture infrastructure resulted in increase in agriculture production by 32% and also an improvement in roads and transportation networks resulted in a 33% increase in household income of the poor. Idriss *et al* (1992), also assert that development of improved appropriate technology can also do the trick of poverty reduction. In fact, Janvry *et al* (2002) and Idriss *et al* (1992), are of the opinion that increased access to credit is an answer to poverty. These scholars argue that providing access to credit and financial services stimulates rural productivity as well as micro enterprise trading and manufacturing.

Chikwanha-Dzenga (1999) argues that the most effective and efficient way to deal with poverty would be for the poor to pool their resources as a group or unofficial club, then use the pooled funds to start a home-based production processes like knitting jerseys or crocheting doilies. She argues that such clubs or societies have caused some individuals with the right business acumen to move to a higher social class even if the profits are not very high. She also points to the psychological aspect when she indicates that it also frees them from a poverty of the mind syndrome that has apparently entrenched its roots amongst the rural folk who have come to accept poverty as a way of life.

IFAD (2004) advocates for provision of basic financial services as a solution to rural poverty. According to IFAD more than a billion poor people lack access to the basic financial services which are essential for them to manage their precarious lives. To them it's important for the poor to have access to credit, to save and to invest so as to provide their families with social safety nets. The poor have been hindered from accessing credits from formal financial institutions due to lack of collateral and also the fact that their loans are too small to attract the financial institutions. IFAD believes that in order to deal effectively with rural poverty microfinance institutions, the government, nongovernmental organisations and credit unions should avail low interest loans to the poor so as to improve their access. This will enable the poor who have the interest and the technical know how to get an opportunity to start microenterprises.

PWPs and stakeholders in poverty alleviation

A stakeholder is a person, group or organisations that have interest or concern in an organisation. Stakeholders can affect or be affected by the actions, as well as policies and objectives of the organisation. Additionally, Swanepoel and De Beer (2000) observe four main stakeholders in rural poverty alleviation which are the public sector (represented by government organs), the private sector, the non-governmental organisations (NGOs) and the popular sector (the local community). The local community according to Swanepoel and De Beer are the most important stakeholders. It was further noted by Novak (1998) that the poor people in the rural areas have the potential to spearhead self-sustainable development. This idea is quite interesting and raises intellectual curiosity. It invokes a mind boggling question: "If the local community has such capability, why does it not simply go ahead with development on its own?"

In response to this question, we note that the government has the key role to play in the development process of any project engaged in the rural areas and elsewhere. Nevertheless, it has been observed that if the priority of the needs is not sorted out with the people, the government may spend millions of dollars on rural development projects that does not satisfy the people's basic necessities. The tendency here is that people in the rural areas, if not directly involved in the projects, they will either work to sabotage the project or simply not

24

cooperate. Following the same line of thought, Swanepoel and De Beers (2000) argue that programmes that fail to derive opinions of the stakeholders in most cases do not yield the desired results. It is therefore worth mentioning that failure to consult local communities in project planning and implementation can lead to the failure of rural PWPs in achieving the desired results.

In Zimbabwe, the government came up with Public Works Programmes as a development policy that was aimed at developing both rural and urban areas. This has been done through the creation of the Ministry of Local Government under Chapter 29 of the Zimbabwean Constitution that came into being in April 1980 and rewritten in 2013. Development is measured by the people's way of life and infrastructural development of the places which they live in. Nevertheless, the Central Statistics Office of Zimbabwe in 2012 reveals that the majority of the rural folk in Zimbabwe live far below the poverty datum line. As such, one wonders whether public works programmes strategy in Zimbabwe is contributing to the reduction of poverty.

A World Bank study shows that in a sample of 14 countries which had adopted the public works strategy, only one showed considerable progress in facing the challenges (FAO 1989). Besides, the study by the World Bank in 2006 indicates that in sub-Saharan Africa the progress of reducing poverty especially in the rural areas is "stubbornly slow". The study has some projected statistics which assume that by 2015, poor health, education, deprivation of productive employment, environmental degradation, bad governance and conflict will be the greatest challenges for sub-Saharan Africa. These challenges will not deepen the rural people's poverty but also compromise the capacity of PWPs in the country to alleviate and worse still to eradicate poverty. It can be further argued that Zimbabwe cannot be totally excluded in this assertion. Hague (2007) notes that misguided policies and maladministration have brought the Zimbabwean economy to the verge of collapse. Although this comment carries overtones of sarcasm, criticism and caricature, we note that there is a problem with public works programmes and other poverty alleviation strategies being employed in Zimbabwe, particularly on how they are implemented and managed.

While the Zimbabwean government has been approaching the issue of poverty through several interventions including public works schemes, it is sad to note that poverty remain topping the rankings among numerous economic and social challenges facing the country. Matunhu (2012) observes that in Zimbabwe, just like in most states in Africa, poverty is predominantly a rural phenomenon. Under these circumstances, one wonders whether the Public Works strategy is misguided, misconstrued or mismanaged. Garnier (2009) notes that public works create employment in the short run and responds to crisis situations. Whether Zimbabwe has realised success for such great expectations raises eyebrows. Given these realities, this raises important questions that can PWPS be an avenue to poverty alleviation in rural Africa in general and Zimbabwe in particular.

Conclusion

This chapter has discussed a number of issues pertaining to poverty in rural Africa. It has underscored that poverty has remained at the centre stage of all the problems that have troubled Africa since colonialism and the birth of the urban environment in Africa. As such, there is need to offer long-term solutions especially in rural Africa which harbour a considerable number of the continent's population. Further, the chapter has noted that the debate on poverty is so complex to the extent that the world in general and Africa in particular is still at crossroads. There is no universally agreed solution as to what can totally eradicate poverty in the rural areas. Over the years, PWPs have evolved as a major policy instrument for creating employment, in the short term, in situations of high, and seasonal, unemployment or underemployment, and for minimising serious income and consumption shortfalls among certain segments of the population in times of crises such as drought and famine. However, although PWPs have been widely advocated and implemented, their impact in terms of poverty alleviation is yet to be seen. The extent to which these programmes have reached and benefited the poor remains shrouded in controversy.

Chapter 2

Theory, Poverty and Development

"Theory has so far proved to be a double-edged sword. It is a double-edged sword that cuts from both ends. While liberating, theory also oppresses as it has done to Africa.... Through foreign theories that African leaders have unwittingly allowed to sprawl obtusely, today, Africa remains locked in the grips of underdevelopment" (Munyaradzi Mawere 2016; 2017: 27).

Introduction

Human development has become one of the most important aspects of the development process, yet this is often impacted by rural poverty. In fact it has become obvious that the two concepts of 'human development' and 'rural poverty' have a close relationship with each other. Therefore, it is important to identify this relationship to overcome the poverty and increase the quality of human development. When the poverty incident is high, it automatically leads to human poverty and adversely affects human development. Most countries in the Global South have paid attention to overcome the problem of poverty since independence. Sadly, quite a considerable amount of the population are still living below the poverty datum line, and many others still wallowing in abject poverty.

Poverty and human development

The concept of poverty has taken centre stage in development discourses since the end of the Second World

War and the beginning of the decolonising project in Africa. Many countries across the globe during the past few decades have made a number of attempts to reduce the world poverty level. This was thought as necessary because the issue of poverty is directly connected to the development paradigms of the world. Many development attempts focus on rural poverty with poverty considered as a key concept.

It has been realised that poverty continues affecting rural human development in many ways. Furthermore, it has been realised that poverty negatively influences the quality of human life. Even though some poor families have participated in poverty alleviation programmes, their situation does not seem to improve at all. If we consider some poor families' history, they have participated in a number of poverty alleviation programmes. But still they have not escaped from their poverty. So there may be a hidden reason for their poverty. Most African governments pay more attention every year to reduce poverty incidents. But the situation change very slowly. When the poverty incident is high, it automatically leads to human poverty and adversely affects human development.

Most importantly, the concept of development was initially viewed from an economic growth perspective. In the 1950s when it first emerged as a global project, development was considered to be synonymous with economic growth; that is if a country's economy was growing, that country was assumed to be experiencing development (cf. Mabogunji, 1980; Thomas, 2000). More than half a century later, the concept of development now encapsulates not only an economic dimension but also social, cultural, political and environmental dimensions and has broadly become human-centred. In short, the objective of development policies and processes has become human development. At the same time, however, and as evidenced by the MDGs, poverty reduction has become the core of the development agenda (Thomas 2000). Indeed, as Thomas (2000) observes, it would now be easy to equate development with poverty reduction, although he stresses that this is a very narrow, restricted definition of development. Nevertheless, the emphasis on poverty reduction is arguably an indication of how significant a challenge poverty is to the achievement of human development.

Besides, the evolution of the meaning of development from simply economic growth to a more complex concept might be attributed to or reflect the process of globalisation which, according to Knutsson (2009), has resulted in a multiplicity of the agents of development and levels of development analysis. Perhaps as a consequence, it remains difficult, if not impossible, to define development precisely although its significance is undoubtedly understood. A consensus is yet to be achieved in terms of a unifying definition. Indeed, such a definition might remain elusive for the many years to come. As Hettne (1995: 15) observes, "there can be no fixed and final definition of development, but only suggestions of what development should be in a particular contexts".

In addition, Sharpley (2015) notes more generally that "development" is an ambiguous term that, on the one hand, can be thought of as a process leading to the condition of economic growth and, on the other hand, a philosophical concept that focuses on a desirable future state. Nevertheless, Thomas (2000) argues that, although attempts to define development within the academic literature have proved to be challenging, revealing inherent complexities and ambiguities in the concept, there is an identifiable path in the evolution of the understanding of development both as a process (that is, 'developing') and an outcome (that is, 'developed').

From an economic perspective, development is the continuous and sustained growth in per capita income. In other words, economic growth and development occur when a country's economic output grows at a rate that is higher than its population growth. Thus, to an economist, the real economic growth rate is a measure of the overall economic well-being of a country's population (Todaro and Smith, 2011). Such economic well-being was, in the initial post-World War Two era of development, equated with development more generally. However, it soon came to be recognised that economic growth alone does not necessarily translate into development for despite enjoying economic growth, many countries still faced significant developmental challenges. As Barbier (1987: 101) argues, "total development' involves more than just 'changes in economic activities' and should include 'political, social and cultural transformations."

More succinctly, for Chambers (2006), development is good change. This implies a positive process or what may be thought of as progress, yet good change may be variously interpreted. For instance, good might refer to positive attributes that are desirable and measurable but change may not necessarily be positive. Rather, it can be a process which may entail disruption, representing challenges to control (Thomas, 2000). The questions to be asked, therefore, are: what is good (change)? And, what constitutes a good change in the context of development?

Evidently, no clear or definite responses to these questions exist; they demand individual reflection, articulation and the sharing of ideas (Chambers, 2004). Nevertheless, one of the first to challenge the development-as-economic-growth perspective was Seers (1969:89) who asked: "What has been happening to poverty? What has been happening to unemployment? What has been happening to inequality?" If all of these are declining then, arguably, development is taking place and, hence, a decline in poverty, unemployment and inequality together might be considered good change. Conversely, Seers (1969) claim that if one or more of these measures is on the increase, then development is not occurring. Seers' approach, however, is narrow as it fails to encapsulate the multi-dimensional nature of poverty. Development refers to an event constituting a new stage in a changing situation or a process of change that is multi-dimensional in nature. In other words, development involves multiple processes and events (Sharpley, 2015) and, significantly, is a dynamic concept or, as Stiglitz (1998: 4) indicates, "it epitomises 'a transformation of society' from traditional relations to more modern ways of doing things".

Usefully, however, Goulet (1992) summarises, development as the good life that embraces at least five dimensions, namely:

i). An economic component- wealth creation and equitable access to resources.

ii). A social component, that is, improvements in health, housing, education and employment.

iii). A political dimension- the issue of human rights and appropriate political systems.

iv). A cultural dimension, that is the protection or affirmation of cultural identity and self-esteem.

v). The full-life paradigm which means the preservation and strengthening of society's symbols, beliefs and meaning systems.

Collectively, these dimensions focus on what may be described as the betterment of the human condition. Development should aim at ensuring the total wellbeing of people within a given society. Indeed, development as currently understood is concerned with political, cultural and economic progress, of course, with social progress at the centre. According to Porter *et al* (2013), social progress is the capacity of a society to meet the basic human needs of its citizens, establish the building blocks that allow citizens and communities to enhance and sustain the quality of their lives, and create the conditions for all individuals to reach their full potential. For Sen (1999), the goal of such social development is simply 'freedom' or, more precisely, the capability of people to achieve their full potential as human beings. Similarly, the United Nation Development Programme (UNDP) has defined it as the ability to live a long, healthy life, the ability to be knowledgeable and ability to have access to the resources needed for a decent standard living (UNDP, 1995). More recently, this social development has been defined of more precisely as human development:

Human development [is] a process of enlarging people's choices. The most critical ones are "to live a long and healthy life, to be educated and to enjoy a decent standard of living. If these essential choices are not available, many other opportunities remain inaccessible" (UNDP, 2010: 10).

Generally, then, the meaning of development has evolved over the last sixty years or so from a narrow, economic growth a defined process to a broad, multi-dimensional concept that is concerned with optimising an individual's well-being. Hence, it arguably involves both tangible, measurable indicators such as wealth, education, life expectancy and so on and also intangible factors, such as an individual's sense of personal fulfilment.

This is not to say, however, that the debate on 'what is development?' has been resolved. As Hettne (2009) suggests, development can only be thought of in terms of particular societies and the ways in which they seek to address their specific developmental challenges. Moreover, it should also be noted that although the concept of development is most frequently considered in the context of developing countries, it is of equal relevance to developed countries. That is, as Sharpley (2015) suggests, a developed society 'does not cease to change or progress. Rather, it is the nature and direction that differ between developed and developing countries. Therefore, development is not limited to only the developing world but remains a global problem.

Not only has development been variously defined but also an understanding of how development occurs (or does not, as the case may be) has been subject to different schools of thought. In other words, different paths to development reflect philosophies that are typically referred to as development theories or paradigms. According to Potter *et al* (2008), development theories are set of rational propositions that seek to explain how development has taken place in the past and should take place in the future. Thus, for Potter *et al*, development theories are either normative, generalising about what the situation should be in an ideal world, or positive when they refer to what is the actual situation.

Development theories

Just as the concept of development has evolved over time, so too have development theories evolved and broadened in scope, from simple economic growth to theories of societal transformation. Development approach is the means of achieving the agenda of advancement which is guided by ideological thought. Consequently, development involves an ideology (the ends) and a strategy (the means) (Hettne, 1995). Development paradigms have been classified in various ways. It is important to take note of the conventional debates surrounding the research in order to put social development in its proper context. The study does not intent to develop new theories but social development will be analysed and assessed as a possible theoretical approach for the development of Africa.

The modernisation theory of development

Modernisation movement is an economic theory of development that is rooted in capitalism and it emphasises that all nations are characterised by modernisation as their ideological model of development. As Haines (2000) notes, modernisation theory assumes that all societies tend to follow one prescribed path to development; hence societies not yet developed are yet to pass through stages passed by the developed countries. Matunhu (2011) points out that, modernisation is about Africa following the development footsteps of Europe (largely the former colonisers of Africa). The theory states that if Africa is to achieve development as that of the so-called developed nations of Europe, it has to pass through all the stages that Europe passed through. Without following these stages, for modernisation theory, Africa can never develop: it will remain poor.

As Rostow suggests in his modernisation theory, the linear stages of growth model he propounded development should follow a linear style with nations emerging from traditional stage and then move to the pre-conditions of take-off, the take off stage, drive to maturity, and the stage of high mass production.. According to the modernisation development theory, the third world poor nations can achieve the same status as their developed counterparts if they would accept modernisation as their goal. Haines (2000) postulates that the modernisation approach promised a guided transition towards a developed industrial society to developing countries. In this regard, development is seen as a global process aimed at producing the image of a highly developed society.

In addition, the structural change model which emphasises the transformation of developing nations' economies from a heavy dependency on subsistence agriculture to urbanised industrial economies from a heavy dependency on subsistence agriculture to urbanised industrial economy is also another modernisation theory. The two sector labour model by Lewis and patterns of development model by Chenerry again falls under modernisation theory. Todaro (1981) notes that, the underdeveloped economies consist of two sectors which are the traditional rural subsistence sector with surplus labour and a second high productivity urban industrial sector that relies on labour from the rural sector. Thus, the core assumption is that transformation of the economy would have occurred when rural labour is transferred to urban centres until it is absorbed in industries.

Criticisms of the modernisation theory

The theory has been criticised for failing to consider the poor as the centre piece in poverty reduction (Matunhu 2011). By ignoring the involvement and participation of the intended beneficiaries, modernisation theoretical approach achieves the marginalisation of poor people and their commitment, initiative and aid to the intervention strategies. Matunhu argues that the strategy becomes an imposed strategy and such a strategy fails to construct adequate notions of both the casual powers of social structures and the role of human agency in shaping social relations in general. The modernisation theory implies that the standard of living is likely to go up as poor countries industrialise (Moyo *et al* 2014). Industrialisation has however had some negative impact on the lives of rural women and children who are left by men to fend themselves.

Another criticism of the modernisation theory is that it is based on deterministic reason which states that within the linear model of socio-economic development, changes are initiated externally. This encouraged foreign powers to prescribe their route to the development of the African continent. In in the 1980s, Africa was a victim of failed Economic Structural Adjustment Programmes (EASP). According to Mlambo (2002), ESAP was dubbed as the Eternal Suffering of the African people. In addition to that, Matunhu (2011) notes that ESAP did not succeed because the programme was imposed and totally disregarded socio-political and the traditional values of the African people. Thus, ESAP failed owing to the fact that it was a European experiment and as a result it failed to pull the continent out of poverty. Another development theory is the basic needs approach which we discuss below.

The basic needs approach to development

The basic needs development strategy became popular in the 1970s. This is when many states became fully aware of the fact that economic development would not address the problems of underdevelopment and that the gap between the rich and the poor is widening at a sporadic pace. According to this theory, human societies should not follow luxurious ways of living. It further stresses that if the focus was on fulfilling "basic needs" of all people, on this planet would have enough resources to meet these needs (Kothari 1993).

As Haines (2000) notes, the basic needs theory is premised in the idea of shifting from a grant theory to more practical approaches aimed at poverty alleviation through the provision of social services like schools and colleges (educational and vocational), as well as hospitals, clinics and welfare programmes. It can be argued that the approach supports the view that no development can take place using the ideas made in isolation of the intended beneficiaries. According to Moyo *et al* (2014), development of the community should begin with the rise of the people at grassroots level towards their own emancipation. The basic needs development approach was the first people centred approach to development.

Criticisms of the basic needs development approach

The main goal of the basic needs development approach is to provide the basic needs of the poor people within a very short space of time. It can, therefore, be noted that this approach was put forward to prove the fact that meeting the needs of the poor people would not only help to reduce poverty but also improve on the education and skills levels of the population: it would empower them as a people.

Nevertheless, the basic needs development approach never developed a methodology on how the basic needs of the people would be met. Besides, the approach focuses on improving public services which is virtually impossible for financially overstretched communities. The basic needs approach eventually lost its appeal in the early 1980s, due to the emergency of a separate approach to ending poverty and enhancing human potential towards the development of poor countries (De Beer and Swanepole 1998).

The neo-liberalism approach to development

Neo-liberalism development approach gained currency in the mid-1970s. The approach favour market liberalism and a competitive market economy. According to this approach, market competition is important and acknowledged as the motive power behind economic growth. As noted by Chani (2008), that neo-liberal scholars believe that market economy is an important ingredient of democracy because by dispersing the ownership of property, it limits the confinement of power in the hands of the law.

Besides, neo-liberals subscribe to the rule of law that is the doctrine that the powers of government should be limited by a higher constitutional law, that the exercise of power should be based on predictable laws rather than discretional commands. They also content that there is a higher command to which governments are subject and which in extreme cases may justify rebellion against dictators. Haines (2000) postulates that the global economic recession of the 1980s, declining commodity prices and mounting third world debt were decisive of this policy shift in third world.

Mlambo (1992) argues that SAPs require the borrowing country to restructure its economy through demand management, currency devaluation, and trade liberalisation, elimination of price controls, and reduction of budget deficit, removal of government subsidies on goods and services and increasing interest rates to their natural market levels to discourage capital flight. It is important to note that, other requirements are that the borrowing country should reduce state investment in the economy, privatise public operations such as government parastatals and the opening up of the local economy to foreign investment.

Criticisms of the neo-liberal approach

The neo-liberal approaches in the structural adjustment era came as a poverty reduction strategy but proved to be against the poor as it destroyed the welfare programmes and cut back on social services. Drawing on the Zimbabwean experience, Mlambo (1992) argues that Economic Structural Adjustment Programme (ESAP) proved disastrous to Zimbabwe given that all the impressive gains and strides made since independence were eroded by the programme. Schuurman (1993a) states that liberalism the effect of destroying welfare programmes and hence poses a disadvantage to the majority poor. A follow-up on neo-liberalism leaves academics doubtful as to who should be players in rural development as it removes the idea of collective ownership of assets and state investment in public institutions. Having noted the failure of the development theories to wipe away poverty in the Global South, scholars have come up with the African renaissance approach (Matunhu 2011; Mawere 2017a).

The African renaissance approach

In Africa, the antithesis to the modernisation theories is the emerging African Renaissance Theory. The African

Renaissance Approach believes that, the attempt to resolve Africa's poverty situation should not be executed from outside but from within Africa. Africa needs homemade strategies to save its people from sinking down into the chasm of poverty and underdevelopment. It is therefore extremely crucial to note that, the African renaissance approach to development is premised on African values of Ubuntu/Unhu, beliefs and norms that are the very building blocks of African life. African life is based on African philosophy and values of unity; communalism and shared purpose of existence which can be a panacea and in fact avenue to true development. Matunhu (2011) concurs that the African renaissance theory advocates for local solutions, pluralism, and community based solutions and reliance on local resources. Poverty reduction measures that have been influenced by the modernistic theories have failed to yield desired results in an African set up. This resonates with Mawere (2017b), who argues that:

> Instead of imposing foreign-made policies on Africa, Africans and their countries need to be first and foremost compensated for enslavement and colonial dispossession and exploitation of the past and present so that they become capacitated to care for their impoverished citizens. In fact, there is need for Euro-American states to account for contemporary global inequalities, let alone to desist from refusing to compensate Africans for the enslavement and colonial dispossession and exploitation they inflicted on Africa (p. 14).

Mawere (2017b) further explains that Africa should solve its development problems using home-developed theories, models and frameworks, with foreign interventions only coming in as complementary, instead of relying on theories,

42

models and frameworks from Europe and the Americas, which are largely inapplicable and in most cases inconsistent with the realities of the African people.

Underdevelopment of Africa is indeed a result of cultural collision between two different development spheres – the Global North and Africa. The former, because of its strategic and technological advantage over Africa, was able to choke and subdue Africa's culture and value system. In the process, Africa lost its right to determine its way to development. The theory argues that the journey to Africa's true liberation comes with disengagement with the Global North in political and economic terms. Agreeably the journey is long and full of hurdles. Despite the risks ahead, Africa has to unite and no fight for a common course. The radical approach to poverty reduction is the African renaissance theory, which takes Africans to be part of the development problem as well as being part of the solution to the continent's underdevelopment. This is no longer the time to cry foul but to act decisively, knowing pretty well that the west has become even more sophisticated in their plan to keep Africa under economic and political bondage. Besides, therefore, for a clear focus, contextualisation and alignment of research, policy and agenda by scholars, researchers, policy makers and governments of Africa.

The failure of development theories in Africa is evident in the failure of SAPs to yield desired results. The Global South is one of the victims of the IMF and World Bank imposed SAPs. Africa in general and Zimbabwe in particular adopted SAPs in the early 1990s with the aim of resuscitating her ailing economy but to no avail.

Conclusion

This chapter has attempted to unveil the nexus between theory, poverty and development. It has noted that where poverty is high, development is adversely affected. The attempt to solve poverty problems has led to the emergence of development theories that were believed to instil and propel development especially in the Global South. The modernisation discourse, neo-liberalism, and the basic needs approach were some of the suggested remedies to the poverty predicament. In this chapter, we critically reviewed all these approaches. From the review, it has been established that mainstream theories had a major weakness of placing too much emphasis on economic development, the simulation of West European designs and aiming towards the reduction of poverty and not its eradication. Worse still, these theories neglected the input by the local people or communities that have to be developed. Basing on these analyses, we have come to the conclusion that people-centred approaches seem to be more plausible and likely to promote sustainable development anchored on social justice, economic growth, and equality (Mawere 2017a).

Chapter 3

People-Centred Public Works Programmes, Poverty and Development

"If people-cantered and well managed, public works programmes can be a springboard for Africa's development and a panacea to the continent's perennial poverty" (Mawere 2017).

Public works programmes

Public works programmes are long-standing development interventions that have grown both increasingly popular and more ambitious in the recent years. They have aided in the development and poverty alleviation agenda of many countries in the Global South through the provision of employment. The popularity of PWPs owes much to their potential 'double dividend. As long as they are people-cantered (or people-driven), public works programmes do not only aim to alleviate poverty and foster growth by transferring income directly to the poor, they are also designed to build and improve the infrastructure and/or deliver other public goods and services at the same time.

PWPs refers to social protection tools used by many governments across the globe in order to curb unemployment and alleviate poverty (Subbarao 2003). In most cases, this is achieved through the employment of local labour and raw materials to create vital physical infrastructure which are usually lacking thereby boosting productivity. The use of labour intensive techniques instead of sophisticated machinery to develop local infrastructure is aimed at creating more jobs per unit of expenditure. These programmes can be successful in terms of targeting poor people, as well as generating short-term employment and income gains for participants. However, there is less evidence in terms of sustainable income gains and the benefit to poor people from assets created (Subbarao 2003).

Most importantly, public works programmes came a long way in the history of development. Freedman (1989) notes that they were used during the great depression by today's industrialised nations to rescue their ailing economies. In this regard, governments used to mobilise and pour their funds into public investment programmes in order to create employment for the people. PWPs act as flagship programme for tackling poverty and vulnerability through employment. In Africa, the public works strategy was in use as early as 1903 where indigenous labour was mobilised for road and dam construction as well as land conversation. Webb (1992) argues that most independent states implemented labour intensive projects in times of drought and famine as a crisis mitigation strategy. Such schemes play a very prominent role of alleviating both chronic and transient poverty (Ravallion 1990).

While most public works programmes in Africa have been used as a mitigation measure in times of drought as well as famine, they were pushed into mainstream policy instruments for employment creation and poverty alleviation ever since the 1970s. It is argued that the schemes help to improve food security and standard of living by creating sustainable employment. The term "sustainable employment" is used here to refer to jobs beyond those generated directly by the programmes themselves, to employment which is likely to persist after a PWPs have ended. When the idea of mobilising indigenous labour to complete tasks that were meant for the government to carry out was adopted in Africa, it was conceived in the modernisation thinking where African societies had to develop in the same way that Europe had recovered from the effects of the great depression.

PWPs can lead to sustainable employment by encouraging more productive investments. This owes to the fact that participants PWPs receive income in exchange for work. This income transfer can affect investment in two ways. First, the additional income enable beneficiaries to accumulate savings, which can later on be used for productive investments. Second, if income transfers are regular and predictable, they could perform an insurance role, thus altering beneficiaries' risk management capacity and willingness to take risks. This could also translate into higher productive investments.

In addition, PWPs can affect sustainable employment as a result of higher wages. PWPs can lead to a change in wage levels in the private sector if the wages paid in the PWPs are higher than the market average. If the programme is large enough, beneficiaries shift their labour from the private sector to the PWPs, leading to a substantial reduction in the supply of labour to the private sector. This puts pressure on employers to raise wages. Wage rises in the private sector could induce employers to use labour-saving technologies, thereby stifling private-sector labour demand and hurting workers without access to the PWPs. In markets with a high concentration of power, however, higher wages paid in a PWPs will not necessarily induce technology shifts nor reduce the private-sector demand for labour. Instead, they could lead to higher wages in other sectors and improve the quality of employment.

More so, PWPs can lead to sustainable employment by developing skills. PWPs can raise skills levels if they include on-the-job or formal training packages. Training should improve the quality of the labour supply. More skills and better quality labour should then translate into better employability and higher earnings.

Lastly, PWPs can lead to sustainable employment by boosting economic activity. PWPs generate and improve public goods and infrastructure. Better infrastructure can increase agricultural output, lower transaction costs and improve market access, thereby raising the profitability of farms and businesses, which should in turn raise labour demand. However, more evidence is also needed to assess the long-term benefits of the infrastructure and public goods generated by the programmes.

PWPs have been implemented in numerous countries with different objectives. Ravallion (1991) argues that in the eighteenth century PWPs were undertaken in times of deprivation and poverty. In this case, individual households were provided with relief support in exchange for labour provision. The World Bank (1990) stresses that during the great depression, PWPs were also implemented in order to contain high levels of unemployment. In South East Asia, PWPs have been undertaken to contain famine in particular and poverty in general. In Southern Africa, PWPs have aimed at the provision of relief (in cash wage or in kind) to targeted disadvantaged groups of individual households on condition that they provide labour to rehabilitate infrastructure in their local communities. PWPs' major thrust is on labour –intensive infrastructure development activities that play a crucial role in the development process of a nation (Ravallion 1991).

Gaude and Watzlawick (1992) observe that infrastructure is one of the major areas of public sector investment in developing nations with construction, as well as, maintenance works accounting for a significant share of gross domestic fixed investment. The nature of these infrastructural investments makes it easy for the government to create unemployment for unskilled labour in rural societies which hitherto have very limited employment chances. Employment programmes were expected to protect the poor and the vulnerable from policy and weather-induced employment and income shortfalls. For example, public works programmes were expanded to serve as drought-relief intervention in Botswana, Ethiopia, and Zimbabwe in the 1980s and early 1990s. The programmes have passed through the stages of evolution from being merely a response to drought and crisis towards being a major policy instrument set at employment creation and poverty reduction (Derjardin, 1996).

What becomes questionable is the realisation that amidst all efforts to intensify public works programmes in Africa in general and Zimbabwe in particular, poverty continues to increase. This leads to some scepticism about the feasibility of the approach. Is it that Zimbabwe is just following a false paradigm that has never succeeded anywhere else in the world? Does Zimbabwe misread the success stories of other countries, if any? Now let us focus on the classification of PWPs.

Classification of PWPs

As Clay (1986) notes, PWPs interventions can be classified basing on the way they address the objectives of employment and income generation to participating individual households and the creation of economic and social capital. Holt (1983) observes that we have relief works which are primarily rapid responses to food insecurity during years of drought and famine. Under this, provisional employment is offered on the creation of local infrastructure and in return the means of survival are provided to the participating vulnerable individual households.

Besides, there are incomes augmenting PWPs often undertaken in response to seasonal fluctuations in income earnings which first and foremost serve as safety nets for those whose income fall below subsistence levels. Be that as it may, we have long term employment generation programmes designed to cater for employment needs among the unemployed, particularly those caught in structural unemployment trap where alternative livelihoods are not there. The last type of PWPs is the infrastructure programme which put much emphasis in the creation of infrastructure rather than income augmentation.

Targeting in PWPs

Targeting of PWPs largely depend on the type of intervention and the relative emphasis in the objectives of the intervention. Nevertheless, apart from the need to develop infrastructure in disadvantaged societies, the PWPs tend to put emphasis on income generation through employment as a poverty alleviation measure. Furthermore, programmes that are premised on poverty alleviation tend to target the rural poor in disadvantaged communities.

In societies where poverty is rampant, it is often problematic to adopt specific targeting criteria for public works employment due to imperfect information about the poor available to implementers of the projects. It was noted by

Ravalion (1991), that the use of the wage rate that is not higher than the minimum wage for PWPs act as self-targeting device that eliminates those that are not poor in the area by targeting those with low reservation wage rates.

Subbaro (1997) opines that while a low wage rate is likely to keep those that are not poor out of these programmes, it is quite authentic to note that, it may result in low transfer earnings per poor participant. In nations with higher inflation rates in which minimum wages are rarely adjusted, the use of minimum wages may not be socially acceptable and may lead to exploitation of the poor and disadvantaged people by the government. Below we turn to the models of PWPs.

Models of PWPs

There are three models of PWPs in Africa namely short-term safety net, longer-term safety net and public works plus. These models are aimed at graduating participants from safety net coverage. We discuss these models in detail in the ensuing sections.

The short-term model

These are designed to provide cash income to self-selected participants in times of need, for example, to augment seasonal income shortages or to respond to nation or region wide shocks such as floods, droughts, or macro-economic downturns (Subbaro *et al* 2013). Owing to the fact that these programmes tend to be designed and implemented at short notice in response to a crisis or sudden shock, they might typically focus on the maintenance of existing community infrastructure assets or the provision of basic new infrastructure such as restoring/maintaining rural roads, soil conservation, afforestation, and social services. Similarly, temporary employment during slack seasons will contribute mainly to income and consumption smoothing, serving as a safety net for households affected by covariate and idiosyncratic shocks. Existing scalable PWPs can be modified in the event of a global economic crisis or severe macro-economic shock that threatens to push marginally poor households below the poverty line. Such households could join the programme, thus preventing an increase in overall poverty. It is worth stressing that short-term programmes are not likely to pull participating households above the poverty threshold, although this may occur for some households. Moreover, short-term programmes do not typically assign other developmental roles to public works such as including a training component.

Long-Term Model

The second model is exemplified by safety net programmes that provide the poorest with a reliable source of income on a labour-intensive activity for a longer period, typically for at least 75–100 days. Some of these programmes run all year round, as in South Africa and Tanzania. The fundamental motive driving such longer-term public works programs is to provide an income that is sufficient for the reduction of chronic poverty. Their outcome is not only temporary employment creation and infrastructural development, but also poverty reduction helping participating households cross the poverty line. These programmes are also very useful in reducing inequalities in societies in the wake of high economic growth, promoting the basic right to work of the poor, who typically do not have a voice in influencing policy decisions. Programmes in the longer-term model also can have positive labour market outcomes by exerting pressure to raise the free market wage rate for unskilled labour.

Public Works Plus Model

These are that go beyond temporary income-generation activities by offering links to employment (for example, through skills training) or access to community and health services (e.g., through existing social assistance programmes, such as health care or nutrition programmes) are in the public works plus model. The aim of such programmes is to help beneficiaries not only in the short term, but also to enable them to actually graduate from poverty. While the effectiveness of public works programmes as a safety net has been well established, the international evidence on public works programmes as an effective active labour market programme is quite limited, and experience with linkages to service provision is only just emerging. The long-term effects of programmes in this model, while interesting and innovative, largely remain to be seen. Although many countries have been reluctant to experiment with the public works plus model because of its complexity and potential for problems in implementation, several different strategies are being tested globally. Several Organisation for Economic Co-operation and Development countries, where public works programmes are sometimes used as employment of last resort, have set quite ambitious goals for public works plus initiatives. For example, in South Africa, participant training and certification are being incorporated into public works programmes. In Argentina and El Salvador, programme beneficiaries are being linked with sectors that may be creating jobs in the future (Subbaro *et al* 2013). In these programmes, participants, while working on public works, receive training in areas/sectors where the scope for hiring new entrants is high so they could graduate and move out of the programme to pick up employment in growing sectors. Elsewhere, programmes are linked to various community services, such as education and health provision for children.

This model has two components that is the public works component and the nutrition component. The public works component aims to create income and assets that improve nutrition and hygiene in the community. The nutrition component targets vulnerable nonworking household members (children and pregnant/lactating women); it encompasses activities such as communication aimed at improving child care practices (including the promotion of breastfeeding), weekly visits by a community health worker to the household, and provision of food supplements during the lean season. Linking the programme's two components reinforces overall goals of employment creation and nutritional improvement and behavioural change.

Determinants of participation in PWPs

The decision to take part or not to take part in PWPs lies within the individual household or individual time allocation model based on relative income that could be earned in a particular activity. The time allocation model postulates that an individual will allocate available time across several activities to maximise utility which is a function of income and individual or household characteristics. Datt and Ravallion (1994) stress that the individual decides to work on a PWP as long as the work exceeds alternative income from other activities. In most African countries, the likelihood of participation increases with the number of adult members in the individual household and the age of participant. Above all, participation usually reduces with the wealth in a family (livestock ownership). Besides, the likelihood to participate also largely depend on income transfers such as remittances and gifts, level of education, weakness of the participants and in villages with higher wages for unskilled labour (Tekla and Asefa 1997). As was revealed during fieldwork, the table below summarises the criteria of screening people who take part in PWPs:

Table 1: Criteria for Screening Extremely Poor Labour (Participants) for PWPs

	Criteria	Score
1	**Typical Sources of Income**	
1.1	Subsistence farming	
1.2	Casual labour	
1.3	Child labour (Do children work to contribute to family income?)	
1.4	Borrowing	
1.5	Begging (depending on kindness of others.	
2	**Asset Possession**	
2.1	No or small livestock	
2.2	Little or no access to land	
2.3	Few or low quality agricultural and farming tools	
2.4	Distress sale of assets	
3	**Housing Situation**	
3.1	Poor housing conditions in view of state of walls/roofs	
3.2	Lack of toilets	
3.3	Lack of basic household appliances such as radio/ televisions	
3.4	Household density(for example more than two persons per room)	
4	**Demography and Health**	
4.1	High dependency ratio (for example household productive members or dependency ratio of more than three.)	
4.2	Household members with a chronic disease	
4.3	No medical cover	
4.4	Low educational status of household (for example no primary education)	
4.5	Isolation (from the community)	
	TOTAL	

Source: *Field Data, April 2015*

Determination of wage rates and forms of payment

The principal benefit received by an individual from participating in PWPs is income earned from the labour service rendered. The determination of the wage rate in PWPs is critical both for targeting and the benefits that the poor generate from their participation but may also have wider implications on the local economy (Subbaro 1997). Mvula (2000) argues that there are numerous other ways to calculate the wage rates in PWPs. Firstly; the lowest wage for people without the necessary skills is mostly used as a maximum wage that that can be paid to those who chooses to participate in public works employment. Subbaro (1997) advocates for a wage rate that is no more than the prevailing market wage rate for unskilled labour. The issue of whether the minimum wage is more or less than the ruling wage rate remains a critical question. Basu (1987) advocates for a wage rate that is consistent with the available budget such that all those who are willing can be employed at that wage. Ravallion (1991) argues that, the wage rate can be set at a higher level, which is considered socially acceptable, although this require a very generous budget and generate less employment.

In any case it is prominent to strike a balance between the objectives of self-targeting and ensuring that the workers receive meaningful transfer. Too low a wage helps to keep the overall participation rate low while simultaneously ensuring a misappropriate number of poor workers than would be observed if the wage rates were higher.

Design and implementation of PWPs

Design and implementation of PWPs refers to the manner in which PWPs are planned, executed, administered and implemented in order for the beneficiary communities to yield the maximum results from them. Table 2 below shows the design and implementation of PWPs.

Table 2: Design and implementation of PWPs

Stages	What you should consider
A).What you need Capital Food/cash Implementing agencies Institutions	Source of financing: if out of general tax revenues, consider competing demands from other public goods. Consider other demands on scarce institutional and administrative sources.
B). Public Work Projects	Choice of projects Community involvement Technical feasibility Labour intensity level of wage rate Mode of payment
C). Immediate impacts Employment	Targeting effectiveness Labour market effects Transfer gains Stabilisation gains Improved risk management Cost effectiveness
Medium-term impacts	Distribution impacts of assets created Second round employment effects Quality of assets Asset maintenance
Other spin offs	Gender impacts Women's empowerment Food security Improved nutrition Community mobilisation

Source: *Karenga (2009: 45)*

Basing on the above, table, it is crucial to commence with the sources and adequacy of financing. If the programme is to be financed out of the general tax revenues, it is useful to consider competing demands for money to generate public goods vital for the general welfare of poor households. Besides, programme need to consider technical feasibility, the level of wage rate as well as the mode of payment, the choice of the project and community involvement. Most importantly, the implication of the choice of the projects and the wage rate on targeting effectiveness in particular and the programme impact in general need to be considered.

Additionally, the potential of the programme to make the incomes stable and reduce the risks faced by poor households needs to be borne in mind. Finally, in terms of impact it is vital to consider the programme effects on income distribution, any second-round employment effects, it may have, any effects on gender gap and its cost effectiveness. Other spin-offs such as community mobilisation, women's empowerment and other social benefits must be put into consideration.

McCord (2003) argues that the implementation of PWPs largely rests on the institutional context in which they are undertaken as well as the social development process in which they are embedded. If PWPs are poorly planned either institutionally or in the social development context, it will be virtually impossible for them to realise their objectives. Howell (2001) came up with tools that can be used in the successful implementation of PWPs. These include goal setting, financial sustainability, integration and partnership building, management, coordination as well as administration. Besides, there is again monitoring and evaluation, governance, politics of the day, accountability as well as corruption of officials. We discuss the tools in detail below:

Goal setting in PWPs
Howell (2001) argues that, it is very important for governments to put in place specific, realistic and achievable

goals and also deciding on what levels of , vulnerability, deprivation of the people and the poverty situation in their country. For instance, according to Alam (2006) the Gonokondra which is regarded as a more focused and well planned poverty alleviation in Bangladesh was very successful as a consequence of its focus on objectives like the improvement in the standard of living in that community.

Financial sustainability

The financial challenges faced by governments usually work against the large scale implementation of PWPs and some cutbacks in government expenditure have again worked against the quality of service provision (Howell 2001). Besides, Howell came up with cost recovery and increased privatisation as remedies. Phillips (2004) adds that, to avert the challenges of financial stability, there is need to introduce a multi-year budget of public works programmes. The Overseas Development Institute (ODI) (2012) again stresses that the cost effectiveness of PWPs is very prominent. PWPs are a more costly method of providing the much needed cash to households as compared to other social protection strategies. This owes much to the need for a lot of capital as well as technical and managerial expenditure precipitated by employment on asset creation. This expenditure can only be less costly if the skills and assets generated by PWPs will play a role in economic benefits and productivity gains for the nation in general and beneficiaries in particular (ODI 2012).

Integration and building of partnerships in PWPs

As Islam (2001) points out, PWPs endeavours to raise the productive and income for the poor rural dwellers. They have the best opportunities of success when they are undertaken within a macro-policy environment which is ideal to their operation. This is corroborated by Philips (2004) who argues opportunities of success when undertaken within a macro-policy environment ensure that adequate resources and time are confined to the planning phase of the PWPs and developing the capacity to ensure effective implementation of the programme.

Howell (2001) argues that there is need to establish partnerships amongst all the stakeholders and stresses that it is more ideal for the implementation and durable sustainability of PWPs. This means partnership between the government, private sector and social welfare organisations should be put in place paying special attention to regulation and facilitation in order to direct the provision. Thus, interaction and partnership ensures more capacity to undertake PWPs at a higher level (Pellisery 2008). The World Bank (1986) recommends that the early involvement of the localities which are intended to benefit from the public works schemes (PWS) is a mandatory obligation. Basing on data harvested from the field in the Zimbabwean rural communities, PWPs are led by the state, NGOs and donor groups as well as the private sector. This can be illustrated by the table below:

State led PWPs

Lead Agent	PW initiatives	Main strategy	Target group	Beneficiary number	Transfer component	Payment
Ministry of Labour and Social Services	Rural Road maintenance, classroom and clinic blocks dip tanks bridge rehabilitation, Urban Grass slashing, Pot hole filling, Sweeping public places	Use of existing legitimate local governance structure	Able-bodied poor and households with elderly, chronically ill, OVC and disabled	Aims to meet annual hunger deficit as highlighted by the ZIMVAC	50kg maize grain when available

cash equivalent (includes local milling costs) | Maize or cash for duration of the programme |
| Ministry of Transport And Infrastructure Development | Contract or Development Programmes through Department of Roads together with ILO | Training of small contractors in labour based technologies. | Local communities where roads were being rehabilitated. | Programme no longer running | Cash for work | Cash for work in line with then ILO standards |

Source: *Fieldwork, April 2015*

NGO and donour led PWPs

Lead Agent	PW Initiatives	Main Strategy	Target Group	Beneficiary Number	Transfer Component	Payment
Oxfam GB as part of the Protracted Relief Programme	Rural Seed and Livestock Vouchers for work	Restocking Agricultural input support	Targeted beneficiary group	3000	$15 voucher	Seed and fertiliser equivalent small livestock, (goats and chickens
USAID Food for Peace (CSAFE)	Rural Dam rehab Construction Community ploughing CF basins Gulley reclamation Irrigation channels	Support to livelihood programming and community works programmes	Non VGF beneficiaries in the community	Varies from site to site and activity to activity but between 100 and 200 individual involved at dam sites.	Food basket	10kg maize, 2kg beans, 750ml cooking oil
UN led A2N and GEF	Rural irrigation development	Community Participatory Development Empowerment approaches	Those already in irrigation schemes and surrounding community	100 to 150 direct beneficiary households per site.	The asset to scheme members and community	Food basket/ cash to casual labourers.

Source: *Fieldwork, April 2015*

Private Sector led PWPs

Lead Agent	PW Initiatives	Main Strategy	Target Group	Beneficiary Number	Transfer Component	Payment
Environment Africa led Industrial Clusters	Local area regeneration and clean ups	Corporate Social Responsibility in operating areas across Harare	Community living and working in and near industrial areas	not known 5 industrial clusters are present in Harare	Clean water Water reticulation systems Energy saving processes	Voluntary – an urban investment structure for PPPs.
Church groups and faith based organisations	Adoption of local police stations and prisons by individual church groups.	Charity and evangelism.	Local communities through church congregations	Not known	Safety and security in the community. Self-reliant prisons.	Voluntary- entry points for further investment and support

Source: *Fieldwork, April 2015*

Community involvement in the selection of the project

Community involvement in the selection of the project is quite vital. First and foremost, it will result in the creation of infrastructure or assets that are most needed by the community. PWPs would then become a genuinely demand driven activity. Furthermore, it creates ownership of the assets created and obviously leads to better maintenance of the asset such as community water outlets. Carlo (2009) notes that it may also help in the site supervision of the project by the community and this contributes to better quality of the asset created. It can be noted that community involvement can be built in into the design of the projects. For instance, sub-project selection could be done at open village meetings or by the elected representatives of the village.

The management, coordination and administration of PWPs

The institutions to manage, coordinate, administer and implement PWPs must be set (Phillips 2004). According to Howell (2002), public works programmes to be more effective require a capable, more competent and accountable administrative system. In this regard, Howell (2002) postulates that governments must put in place a consistent and transparent evaluation system and again monitor the progress of PWS quarterly or annually. The process embraces equitable, democratic, and participatory values. In the case of PWPs in Zimbabwe, although local government has, the ability to carry out this process, both in-depth accounts gathered through focus group discussion and interviews in the field testified the use of community-based processes of worker selection.

Basing on fieldwork data, we observed that in one method, all villagers wanting work put their names in a hat and names were selected in an open meeting, with the committee overseeing the process. Names selected from the hat became the final list of people to take part in the public works project. Nevertheless, if a name of a person who had employment elsewhere came up, the person was asked to withdraw, and if more than one name per family was selected, one of them was withdrawn and a new name selected from the hat again. Another method involved putting the names of those wanting work on a list at a community meeting and a consensus reached on who should get the jobs. This was also considered a community process because selection criteria had been decided at a public meeting. The community members feel they are making equitable decisions based on need. The villagers defended their position by arguing that they know who deserves to be given employment from their villages. They argued that it is easy to reach consensus on who should be helped. Usually by the time jobs become available, villagers would have already decided on which household needs assistance of what kind to survive.

Monitoring and Evaluation of PWPs

Philips (2004) advocates for an effective monitoring and evaluation (M&E) of PWs. This is a quite significant aspect to make sure that PWS is achieving the objectives it is meant to achieve. Monitoring and Evaluation according to Kusek and Rist (2004) helps to build greater transparency and accountability that is resource utilisation and improve project planning and development. The Monitoring and Evaluation aspect therefore cannot come at the end of the planning process but it cuts in almost every phase of the programme and project planning. For instance, it is a prominent requirement to monitor whether the benefits of the PWPs are reaching the intended beneficiaries (Howell 2002). According to McCord (2003), Monitoring and Evaluation is vital in the collection of data and baseline information about the impact of PWPs.

Governance, politics of accountability and corruption in PWPs

As argued by Phillips (2004), for PWS to be successful and to attain the desired outcomes, political support is a basic requirement. Nevertheless, the bad aspect of this is that PWS are normally associated with the ruling clique or political figures as a consequence of the government claim of generating employment for their citizens. A study of emergency employment programmes in Argentina found out that politics itself had a hand in the targeting of beneficiaries and that these programmes were manipulated by political figures owing to the fact that they were not conducted with clients or beneficiaries at heart (Giraud 2007).

Basing on the information we harvested from the field, some participants in the focus group discussions felt that there are some rowdy elements among those in need of employment. These were supposed to be punished by exclusion from milking the benefits coming to the community. Further probing established that their unruliness was in the form of holding political sentiments divergent from the rest of the community. This is a shortcoming of public participation in deciding who must get jobs. The criteria may end up being manipulated (or politicised) and going at odds with participatory development and social development objectives.

Apart from this weakness, both focus group discussants and household interviewees criticised the same decision-making processes as slow, difficult, and sometimes unfair because of difficulty in distinguishing and describing who is the poorest of the poor. People sometimes do not want to agree on who the poorest of the poor are. Poverty targeting perspectives on equity claim that the poorest of the poor should get jobs. For example, the hat system implies that everyone gets an equal chance. This poses a threat of potential tension between the democratic participatory principles and poverty alleviation objectives as some better off are picked from the hat in a democratic process. Some community members felt more satisfied with this random rather than purposive, targeted selection others felt it left out some very needy people although it is a fair practice.

To the researchers, the citing of nepotism, despite the general feeling that the process was fair, generated the feeling that community structures must have nothing to do with employing and firing people because that puts them exactly in conflict with their own communities. It creates community war against itself. What they have to do is to be part of the decision making process in terms of what projects must be run and how must they be run and how should the community benefit. On the part of taking those structures and making them part of the recruiting process, it creates problems of hatred as revealed during fieldwork.

Nevertheless, the selection process unveiled is a good example of a people-centred participatory process. It encompasses democratic decentralisation values that form the foundations of public works philosophy. UNCDF (2003) stresses that poverty can be reduced if government policy is more responsive to the people's needs and initiatives. The data implies that there are better responses to local needs, with local authorities tending to act more in line with local preferences and conditions. Public works projects have better chances of being sustainable since local people are more involved in their design, execution, and monitoring. The system minimises the prevalence of corruption while increasing transparency, responsibility and accountability, which are in fact key to sustainable development and success of any project. Popular participation also decreases chances of sabotage by the local people since they do not isolate themselves from the projects.

Why governments undertake PWPs

There are numerous reasons why countries undertake PWPs. PWPs are implemented with the objective of providing to poor households a source of income by creating short term employment. Besides, PWPs also help to achieve complementary objectives of creating public goods for the community which may in turn lead to secondary employment and income benefits. We discuss some of the reasons in detail in the sections that follow.

PWPs as mitigation for covariate shocks
Carlo *et al* (2000) argues that PWPs provide an income transfer via wages to smooth consumption of poor households in the wake of a major shock such as economic meltdown(including stabilisation programmes or other reforms causing sharp rise in unemployment and income) or natural disasters like floods, drought or in times of a poor agricultural season. Above all, third world countries do not have formal unemployment insurance programmes for a variety of reasons which include feasibility (underdeveloped

financial markets) and inability to finance the projects. In these countries, public works programmes run at a sporadic pace after the occurrence of the crisis or a few months in a year and then scale down in better times, for example, during seasons when people receive good rains and bump harvest.

PWPs as mitigation for idiosyncratic shocks (insurance guarantee)

In this pretext, the main objective is to guarantee employment at a low wage demanded by workers. In other words, workers would enjoy the leverage to move in (when market wage is low) and out when the market wage is higher than the public works wage. Wilclock (2009) opines that, in countries where there is no formal employment insurance, public works programmes are capable of performing an insurance role.

A bridge to employment

PWPs may include a training aspect on top of the income transfer to help workers in the acquisition of skills needed to gain more permanent employment or able to do piece jobs. The other requirements needed for workers may include saving some of their wage earnings, learning technical skills and eventually obtain a credit and begin an activity other programmes have explicit training component thereby enabling workers to acquire the needed skills to transition into a more regular empowerment (Carlo 2009).

As a poverty alleviation strategy

The major objective of public works programmes is mainly that of poverty alleviation through labour absorption. PWPs provide substantive income support to poor households in those nations with a huge segment of poor unemployed people. PWPs can not necessarily absorb all the jobless people in the society but add to the range of initiatives to address the challenges of unemployment. As McCord (2012) argues, numerous governments try to overcome employment challenges by spending money in the generation of public assets through labour intensive methods. In fact, it can be noted that against that background, PWPs are undertaken throughout the year and are also likely to engage people for a longer period of time (Mvula 2000). Besides, the Overseas Development Institute (2012) stresses that public works programmes are sometimes used as social protection strategy to address the needs of the working age poor. They are expected to lessen dependency on social protection and play a pivotal role in the economic development of a country. Additionally, Samson and Niekerk (2006) stress that, public works programmes appeal to policy makers in four main ways.

First, vulnerable groups are less susceptible to dependency through public works programmes. This is in line with the ideology of not giving beneficiaries something for something. Second, it was also deduced that public works programmes precipitate the creation of employment by providing a "win – win" combination of welfare transfers and the creation of productive assets. Third, it may again be noted that the creation of productive assets helps in attaining the growth objectives of the government and poverty alleviation as well. Lastly, the low wage rates of PWPs efficiently target the poorest of the poor which in actual fact ensures that social protection is provided to the vulnerable groups especially those in rural areas thereby playing a pivotal role in poverty alleviation.

However, PWPs are in most cases regarded as a short-term emergency strategy to cyclical shock in labour markets and are not generally considered as a suitable response in addressing structural employment challenges and chronic poverty (Kostze *et al* 2010). Be that as it may, the varying success of public works programmes around the world is mainly due to variations in their design features and the implementation methodology (Howell 2003). It is interesting to note that the assertion is identical to McCord's perspective that the achievement of the objectives of public works programmes relies much on the institutional capacity for implementation and the addition of social development considerations to PWPs that are conceived and executed.

In sub-Saharan Africa, where food insecurity and poverty both in rural and urban areas is evident, PWPs have played a crucial role as a poverty alleviation strategy. With financial support from donors, most governments have launched production safety net programmes. This refers to PWPs that contribute to improving the productive and efficiency of transfers to food insecure households, reducing household vulnerability, improving resilience to shocks through multi-year predictable resources rather than through a system dominated by emergency humanitarian aid (Karenga 2009).

For Carlo *et al* (2009), the anti-poverty objective does not motivate workfare programmes only in developing nations but also the developed ones facing structural unemployment challenges, especially widespread among third world countries. In these countries, the anti-poverty objective is intended to provide income assistance to the poor, as the state's levels of income increases, a public work programme is still intended to help the poor but its focus is different such as countering a situation of structural or rising unemployment or to help specific fragments of the population.

PWPs generate durable assets which can improve the standards of living of rural communities where they have been implemented (Carlo *et al* 2009). The infrastructure can lead to local economic growth, creation of jobs and alleviation of poverty. Some PWPs were targeted on relief where as others endeavour to create employment. The output of such programmes is twofold, that is, to increase the income earnings of the beneficiary communities and the creation of public goods such as new infrastructure or the improvement of existing infrastructure or service delivery. Besides, PWPs with a variety of aims such as protecting people from large covariate shocks (for example, floods and famine), to protect rural people especially if they lost their jobs, fight against poverty.

We add that, PWPs have played an important role in fragile countries coming out of years of conflict. These countries face severe development challenges such as weak institutional capacity, bad governance, as well as political instability and political violence and street fighting (Carlo, 2009). Therefore, for the said countries to effectively deal with these challenges, several fragile states are using Public Works as a poverty alleviation strategy. Countries such as Sierra Leone successfully implemented PWPs soon after a civil war (1991-2002), in order to rebuild infrastructure damaged soon after the war.

Besides, PWPs can play a pivotal role in reducing and mitigating the risk of changes in climate by generating environmentally friendly public assets. Wilcock (2009) argues that, some of the assets generated can increase the resilience of the societies like water storage and embankments. Not only that, other projects such as forestation and soil conservation projects can help to protect the environment from the diverse impact of changes in climate. Be that as it may, it is important to note that projects which helps to conserve the soil were carried out in semi-arid environments have been instrumental in slowing down the desertification, erosion and creating new forest areas.

Successes of PWPs

In line with the principal objectives of the PWPs, immediate results can be observed on participating households and communities. PWPs can have some positive impacts on incomes through the provision of employment to poor households and individual participating in the public works projects. Owing to this reason, many countries have integrated PWPs in their poverty alleviation programmes. The extent of the impact on poverty depends nevertheless on the wage rate, the timing of the programme, the social benefits of the project and costs associated with the forgone opportunities (Datt and Ravallion, 1994). The empirical evidence on the positive employment and net income effects on participant in PWPs in Global South is quite noticeable. One can argue that access of poor households to PWPs employment appear to improve their net income and lessen poverty burden among the rural poor.

Besides the second and most vital direct effect of PWPs is the development of the physical infrastructure in rural areas by communities. These physical infrastructures include road networks, construction of bridge as well as, irrigation facilities and water storage tanks. Carlo *et al* (2009) note that the availability of these facilities uplifts the social status of the communities and promotes rural development that is necessary for durable and sustainable livelihoods.

The two direct impacts of PWPs generate indirect benefits and costs that have to be that have to be captured in the beneficiary assessment. Wilcock (2009) observes that PWPs can have what we call a "multiplier employment effect" in the local economy in the long run, particularly where the incomes saved are invested in further activities that are economically sound and again productive. It is of great significance to note that some of PWPs may impart skills to the participants in the form of management and organisation work as well as skills in construction activities.

The incomes gained from public works employment can again be used to buy food requirements and this helps to improve the nutritional status of the participating individual households. In addition to that, socially reduction in poverty improves social wellbeing by limiting situations of helplessness and by stabilising the incomes of the poor. Mvula (2000) argues that the development of infrastructure in rural areas may create a favourable atmosphere for productive and economic activities. For example, the construction of a road that links the rural area to market centres may encourage on farm production and agriculture based public works like irrigation and soil conservation are likely to impact positively on agricultural productivity.

In addition, Moyo *et al* (2014) stress that although PWPs have some demerits, they are largely associated with benefits warmly embraced by rural beneficiaries. Drawing insights from Zimbabwe, the rural folk rely on the public works for household incomes and household food source. Be that as it may, PWPs are very useful as a poverty alleviation strategy as they increase household food security and cash flow as well. It is also worth mentioning that cash flows would allow beneficiaries to spend their incomes on any combination of food and other needs of their choice. In the event that they are given money, it means that income would be assured to the most vulnerable while encouraging able bodied men and women to be gainfully employed. It promotes the incentive to work and would eliminate the tendency to continually depend on aid.

PWPs can help beneficiaries to develop skills which can be of great use to them even when the life span of the projects expires. This is because of the fact that some PWPs have a training aspect where beneficiaries can get valuable skills at the full expense of the entire programme. When the project ends, the beneficiaries will be able to use the skills and be gainfully employed in other sectors of the economy.

Basing on field data, women were the main beneficiaries to these programmes. This is hailed as it promotes a culture of gender sensitivity. Generally, providing work for rural women has seen more benefits trickling into the households as compared to providing work for men. This is because most of the income is used for household use, which rarely occurs with most men who reduce their families to poverty by using the money on beer. The involvement and participation of women in the decision-making process has also been instrumental, as it has seen the suggestion of very useful projects. Infrastructure like village tracks and water weirs have helped to reduce the day-to-day hardships faced by these women and their communities at large.

The creation of water storage facilities like dams and weirs created a good platform for self-sufficiency as gardening activities could be carried out. The projects played an instrumental role in the expansion and development of rural road network. These roads are very important to the general development of the rural areas, which is strongly linked with poverty reduction. However, relative neglect of the created infrastructure created militated against the comprehensive harvests of benefits brought therewith.

Possible shortfalls of PWPs

While the PWPs have been hailed for the positive outcomes, it appears they are burdened with a load of negative outcomes as well. Of the outstanding negative outcomes, PWPs have been criticised of micro focusing. Few people end up benefiting from the programmes, which pay little dividends. The reduction of food payments to mere tokens of appreciation has been defended as a targeting method to encourage self-selection and discourage the well to do from entering the programmes.

The above means that, only those in need end up participating. This increases poverty as the people will spend valuable time on a poorly paying job that consumes their time, which could be utilised in other activities that can increase their incomes. However, this reduction in the amounts paid off to individuals has been praised as it increases the number of participants in the programmes. This does not reduce poverty but equalises poverty with every person having an equal share with the other while remaining deprived.

The choice of assets in public works schemes has tended to be poor because of public participation. This is connected to poor literacy of the beneficiaries, which can be confirmed by the educational levels attained. The same goes with the lifespan of the assets, which is heavily dependent on the importance attached by the community. This has seriously affected poverty reduction as it ends up not being realised because the assets will have been poorly managed hence trickle down ends up not happening.

Overwhelming was the criticism on corruption. Public participation with community leaders being in charge increases the grip of the community on the projects. This, however, has been criticised to be one factor increasing corruption. With the low levels of literacy, inequitable power structures allow corruption to flourish.

It was also realised that no long-term employment has been generated and no effort towards doing this has been exerted. It was learnt that there is too little or no training that is associated with the programmes hence no building of capacity to get formally employed. This was concluded to be one reason why the people of rural Zimbabwe remain deprived of employment. They are technically handicapped and programmes do little to foster their emancipation.

Poverty persists in the district because public works aims at curing symptoms of poverty. There is no effort at transforming the present conditions but emphasis is laid on improving the situation, which ends up in an equalisation of poverty among the poor communities. This means that poverty remains in place but with little inequalities if the poor people are compared.

Many of the projects and assets are neglected as soon as the programme directors leave. Funding also stops coming towards the projects. This has been associated with politicisation of programmes where projects come as campaign tools. After elections, they disappear. In this respect, there is need for self-regenerating and self-financing projects. It can therefore be concluded that although the public works programmes have not been significantly active at reducing some effects of poverty in the study district, they were also instrumental as they brought some useful outcomes.

Conclusion

As discussed in this chapter, PWPs if properly managed can help to eradicate poverty and propel development in Africa. They can positively impact productivity and socio-economic growth through three main channels: i). Cash transfer, ii). assets creation or improvement, and iii). skills development or enhancement. Most importantly, some of the benefits of PWPs include the creation of short-term employment, the provision of much needed food to the rural people, provision of income which has been used for several purposes, and the creation of infrastructure. Besides, the projects aligned to PWPs have a potential of reducing social exclusion while emancipating the poor and previously marginalised societies. Despite all these positive outcomes, it was however revealed that public works programmes have their own shortcomings. When the idea of PWPs was adopted in Africa, it was conceived in modernisation thinking, where African society had to develop the same way that Europe had recovered from the scourge of the Great Depression during the first half of the 20th Century. What becomes questionable is the realisation that amidst all efforts to intensify public works programmes in Africa, poverty continues to increase. This leads to some scepticism about the feasibility of the approach. Is it that Africa is just following a false paradigm that has never succeeded anywhere else in the world? Does Africa misread the success stories of other countries, if any? Out of all this questioning and analysis, we realised that public works philosophy of decentralisation does little to enhance the level of rural people's participation during policy formulation and implementation as intended beneficiaries of PWPs. From the standpoint of social development, public works philosophy can be openly criticised for making economic growth the centre of development. It neglects the human being and puts him second after growth through the creation of infrastructure. Thus, unless these shortfalls are corrected, public works programmes can never alleviate and worse still eradicate poverty in Africa.

Chapter 4

Bridging the Gap between the Poor and the Rich through Public Works Programmes in Africa: Some Case Studies

"Bridges are built for easier access, of which, public works programmes are a bridge and gate pass for the poor into the world of riches so long the people are put at the centre" (Mawere 2017)

Introduction

PWPs have become a long-standing development interventions that have grown both increasingly popular and more prominent in the Global South. Public works is a social protection tool used by governments in developing countries to curb unemployment and alleviate poverty. This is achieved through the employment of local labour and raw materials to create vital physical infrastructure which are usually lacking thereby boosting productivity. The use of labour intensive techniques instead of sophisticated machinery to develop local infrastructure is aimed at creating more jobs per unit of expenditure. This chapter demonstrates how public works programme can act as a bridge between the poor and the rich.

PWPs as development intervention

Generally speaking, in Africa, PWPs have been originally used as strategies poverty relief in response to economic downturns and natural disasters. More recently, they are now used more and more as long-term social protection tools. Generally speaking, the popularity of PWPs is due to their potential to alleviate poverty and foster growth by transferring income directly to the poor people. Most importantly, PWPs are also designed to build and improve the infrastructure and/or deliver other public goods and services.

PWPs can help to alleviate poverty by creating sustainable employment. In Africa, participants in PWPs receive income in exchange for work. This income transfer can affect investment in two ways. First, the additional income enables households to accumulate savings, which can ultimately be used for productive investments. Second, if income transfers are regular and predictable, they could perform an insurance role, thus altering participants' risk management capacity and willingness to take risks. This could also translate into higher productive investments. These additional investments might increase agricultural output, create more business opportunities and, thus, affect employment.

Second, PWPs can affect sustainable employment as a result of higher wages. PWPs can lead to a change in wage levels in the private sector if the wages paid in the PWPs are higher than the market average. If the programme is large enough, beneficiaries shift their labour from the private sector to the PWPs, leading to a substantial reduction in the supply of labour to the private sector. This puts pressure on employers to raise wages leading to poverty reduction.

Third, PWPs can lead to sustainable employment by developing skills. PWPs can raise skills levels if they include on-the-job or formal training packages. Training should improve the quality of the labour supply. More skills and better quality labour should then translate into better employability and higher earnings.

Fourth, PWPs can lead to sustainable employment by boosting economic activity. Public Works Programmes generate and improve public goods and infrastructure. Better infrastructure can increase agricultural output, lower transaction costs and improve market access, thereby raising the profitability of farms and businesses, which should in turn raise labour demand. Studies have shown that, PWPs have provided employment for millions of people in countries such as Rwanda, Tanzania and Zimbabwe (McCord and Farrington 2008; Martens 1989; Manamela 1993; Samson *et al* 2006; Howell 2003; Karenga 1996; Moyo *et al* 2014).

Tanzania's experiences with PWPs

Tanzania soon after independence in 1961 and years up to 2000 was classified as one of the poorest countries in the world. This classification is based on a wide range of monetary indices like Gross Domestic Product (GDP) and Gross National Product (GNP), per capita and living on less than one US dollar per day (URT, 2003). As of 2001, it was found that more than a third of the Tanzanian population could not satisfy their basic needs, and nearly 18 % could not afford to attain food requirements for a healthy living (URT, 2002). Poverty has been growing in spite of the measures being taken by the government and other stakeholders.

Income poverty is still a common feature of the Tanzanian economy. The Household Budget Survey of 2000/01 deduced that, the proportion of the population below the national food poverty line is 18.7% and that below the national basic needs poverty line is 35.7% (URT, 2005b). Most importantly, the World Bank (2000) revealed that about half of all Tanzanians are basically poor and one third is living in abject poverty. Out of this number, between 15 million and 18 million live below poverty line of USD 0.65 a day. Out of these, nearly 12.5 million live in abject poverty, spending less than USD 0.5 a day. Furthermore, the number of people living in absolute poverty has increased because of the rapid population growth. Poverty has been growing in spite of the measures being taken by the government and other stakeholders. The country's economy is heavily dependent on the agricultural sector which constitutes about 50% of Gross Domestic Product (GDP). The sector is a source of employment for about 80% of the population and accounts for 70% of the total exports, 60% of the export earnings and 90% of food crops (Kapinga 2003). Currently, fast growing sectors include mining and quarrying (13.9 %), construction (8.4%) followed by business hotels and restaurants as related to tourism (96.5 %). Lastly, the informal sector is also becoming an important source of employment (URT, 2003). Given the nature and situation of poverty in Tanzania, the speed of alleviating poverty is still slow. As Makombe *et al.* (1991) and Samwel (2004) argue, there has not been any significant achievement in poverty reduction and the actual number of people living in both below basic needs and food poverty has been increasing.

In an attempt to alleviate poverty, the government introduced quite a number of policies. These include Tanzania Development Vision 2025, the National Poverty Eradication Strategy (NPES); Tanzania Assistance Strategy (TAS); Tanzanian Social Action Fund (TASAF), Public Expenditure Reviews (PER), and Medium Term Expenditure Framework (MTEF Poverty Reduction Strategy (PRS); and the National Strategy for Growth and Reduction of Poverty (NSGRP) or MKUKUTA and PWPs (URT 2002).

PWPs in Tanzania

Tanzania's PWPs represents major donor-driven experimentation in Africa to generate employment and create assets. Labour intensive PWPs in Tanzania date back to 1978, with the beginning of the Tanzanian special public works. These programmes included projects that focus on improving rural access roads for instance, the Rukwa and Ruvuma projects. In addition, the Tanzanian PWPS also included flood control and rehabilitation of irrigation projects such as the Arusha and Dodoma projects, afforestation for example the Ruvuma and Dodoma projects, water supply for example the Rukwa Project, and construction of rural housing, that is, the Ruvuma Construction Project.

Important to note is that PWPs in Tanzania aimed to ensure enhanced government support to poor communities, the empowerment of communities through giving them more voice in taking charge of their own development, and stimulation of community demand and the eventual contribution to economic growth, reduction of poverty and protection of vulnerable groups thus leading to improved livelihood of the people. Tanzania has adopted PWPs strategies to involve the people in decision making in the implementation of various projects decided upon by the people themselves. As Mkapa (2001) observes, PWPs are a beacon of hope to Tanzania, and it is determined to fight poverty because of the fact that the PWPs implementation modality motivates people into becoming self-employed. Apart from rekindling the spirit of self-development, the PWPs implementation framework guarantees sustainability because of high degree of ownership.

The design of PWPs in Tanzania

PWPs in Tanzania share a common set of goals. These include:

i).to rehabilitate and maintain rural assets such as feeder roads, irrigation works, afforestation, and piped water supply.

ii).to create employment opportunities for the rural unemployed and underemployed.

iii). to provide supplementary income, particularly for low-income households.

iv). to build the technical and institutional capacity for future replication of labour intensive public works programmes.

Most importantly, the alleviation of poverty is not explicitly featured in these projects, except in the stipulation of a gender balance in employment. Besides, the relative weights attached to these goals are not stated but there is an apparent focus on the creation of employment. The goal of employment creation is not necessarily linked to the generation of income for workers. The projects, especially housing projects, are often considered self-help as opposed to paid labour. Employment is open to adults who are eligible for work. Initial selection is done at the village level. Involvement of the village government is often sought to ensure availability of labour for project work and equitable sharing of paid project work among the village population.

Role of Tanzanian PWPs in poverty alleviation

PWPs in Tanzania were established by the government with the aim of poverty alleviation. These PWPs were designed to address community social needs, targeting the vulnerable groups, intending to improve basic social and economic services. Therefore, PWPs in Tanzania supports community demand driven initiatives that improve accessibility to and delivery of socio- economic services as well as enhancing communities' capacity and involvement of other stakeholders in the whole process. Poverty alleviation activities would be possible if the community development facilitators are engaged in collective decision making and participatory planning. This builds self-confidence and commitment.

Besides, contribution of these projects to total employment is of great significance. Employment in these PWPs ranks as at least the third most important source of income in these villages. Besides, these programmes have managed to address community social needs since they target the vulnerable groups. By and large, the PWPs as a whole have created close to 2.9 million paid jobs. Road projects absorbed 46 percent of the paid unskilled labour in 1980-86 (the Ruvuma road project alone employed 37.3 %), followed by the irrigation projects, which accounted for nearly 40 percent. Forestry accounted for 10.5 percent in 1980-86, but its share expanded to 25 percent in 1987-90, especially with the Bareko project in Dodoma (Martens, 1989).

PWPs and attempts at poverty alleviation in Rwanda

The Rwanda case represents a more advanced experiment with PWPs in Africa. Interestingly, PWPs such as the ones in Rwanda are integral components of the country's national development planning framework. The PWPs in Rwanda expand in times of drought to generate temporary employment for households experiencing drought-induced income shortfalls. Most importantly, Rwanda's PWPs, focuses on the Vision 2020 Umurenge Programme (VUP), one of three flagship programs under the government's Economic Development and Poverty Reduction Strategy 2008–12. It can be noted that Rwanda is an excellent example of a country that has faced some of the most common challenges in wage setting, in particular, the calibration of an efficient wage level that is, one that promotes self-selection among poor beneficiaries and does not distort the local labour market (Subbaro *et al* 2013). With the country's long history of PWPs, Rwanda's wage setting policy has evolved over time, ultimately achieving a consensus and adoption of efficient wage levels conforming to international good practice, leading to poverty alleviation in the country.

PWPs in Rwanda are driven by a demand for the creation of productive assets and the generation of employment on the part of national planners and donors at the national level. Income generated through creation, utilisation, and maintenance of public goods is linked to improved household food security. The food security outcome is conditioned by the public policy environment, particularly employment and wage policies as well as the functioning of the labour market. In addition, PWPs in Rwanda have multiple goals. They are used as a vehicle for the provision of employment (to stabilise intra-year or inter-year fluctuations in employment). They are also an instrument to transfer employment and income to poor segments of the population, guided by a preferred poverty measure (to reduce the incidence of poverty or its intensity). And finally, such programmes are used as a low-cost method of producing rural assets that promote long-term growth.

General background of PWPs in Rwanda

Rwanda is known as the land of Thousand Hills. It is a small land-locked country of 26,338 square kilometres, of which over 96 % is land. Besides, Rwanda is densely settled, with a population of 10.2 million. Generally, close to forty-five percent of the land is dedicated to agriculture, and agricultural work predominates, with approximately 72 percent of the population living in rural communities. Over 85 % of the working population is involved in agricultural activities, and the agricultural sector accounted for about a third of the country's overall gross domestic product (GDP) in fiscal year 2009/10 (NISR 2011). The population density and high population growth rate mean that landholdings are typically small; these average less than a hectare per person. As a consequence, agricultural production tends to be on a subsistence basis. The hilly terrain negatively affects the land's agricultural productivity. Rwanda's rainy seasons are February to April and November to January.

The country's troubled history has resulted in a significant proportion of the working-age population lacking formal education, restricting their ability to access better-paying work. This limitation particularly affects the rural population, which already has little access to work opportunities outside the agricultural sector. Consequently, the rural population is highly dependent on subsistence agriculture to support their families, sometimes supplemented by casual work (petty trade, farm labour etc.). It is against this background that the government of Rwanda has used PWPs as a means of providing poor families with wage-earning opportunities while creating and rehabilitating community assets, generally of an infrastructural nature.

Early experiences with PWPs

Rwanda has been implementing PWPs for the past thirty years as an anti-poverty strategy. Quite a number of donor partners have implemented PWPs, albeit with differing wage rates, objectives, and target groups as shown on the table below:

Table 1: Institutional structure in Rwanda

Provinces	5
Districts	30
Imirege (sectors)	416
Akagari (cells)	2148
Umdugudu (villages)	14831

Source: *Government of Rwanda, 2007*

More so, the first of these PWPs, the pilot Labour-Intensive Special Public Works Programme, was formulated in 1978 and implemented in 1980. It received funding from the government of the Netherlands over a period of three years. Besides, the PWPs in Rwanda received support from International Labour Organisation (ILO). The program was expanded for two implementation phases through 1991, with continuing support from the Netherlands as well as from Austria, Italy, and the United Nations Development Programme.

Works were carried out mainly in the provinces of Gitarama and Ruhengeri, and the overall programme was implemented by the Ministry of Internal Security. In 1991, the Programme National *d'Actions Sociales* (Social Action National Program) was developed to take over from the pilot programme. The new program was implemented in two phases lasting until 1998 by the Ministry of Planning, with financial support from the United Nations Development Programme and the World Bank. Rwanda next developed PWPs in 2002 to address the urgent need of quickly reabsorbing the half-million unemployed and underemployed people in the country's rural areas. The programme was devised to target specific vulnerable groups including ex-combatants (50 percent) and female victims of genocide (50 percent), demobilised soldiers, militia, and detainees. Featuring infrastructure and service projects, the new programme, Programme de *Développement Local à Haute Intensité de Main-d'Oeuvre* (Local Development Programme: Labour Intensive Approach—PDL-HIMO), was designed. The programme was launched in November 2003, with support from the ILO. Shortly thereafter, the Cabinet adopted the Labour Intensive Public Works Strategy.

PWPs under the Vision 2020 Umurenge Programme (VUP) in Rwanda

In 2007, despite remarkable economic growth since 2000/01, a large proportion of Rwandans still lived in extreme poverty. It became clear that unless action was taken, the country's aspirations regarding poverty alleviation would not be achieved. In response, the government in 2007 developed the VUP during its annual retreat. VUP is a broad national social protection programme aimed at reducing the country's rate of extreme poverty from 36.9 percent in 2007 to 24 percent by 2012.2 VUP was launched under the Economic Development and Poverty Reduction Strategy 2008–12; it consists of three components, one of which is the PWPs.

While this component kept a focus on labour-intensive techniques, it also emphasised community-based participatory approaches to build community assets and create off-farm employment infrastructure. The public works component under VUP is complemented by a direct support component to improve access to social services for labour-constrained households, as well as a financial inclusion component to promote entrepreneurship and employment. The design of the VUP public works programme was informed and enriched by Rwanda's previous experience, encompassing a focus on labour-intensive approaches to asset creation, the role of community participation, and the centrality of wage setting to ensure good targeting performance.

Launched in February 2008 in a single sector per district, by 2009, the public works component was scaled up to two sectors per district. As of July 2010, the VUP public works component, together with its direct support component, had been scaled up to 90 sectors, 3 per district. By July 2011, it had been scaled up to 120 sectors, 4 per district. The scale-up plan envisages that all sectors in the country will be covered for direct support by 2016; by that time, 240 sectors will have been reached for public works.

Design issues in Rwanda's PWP

Wage setting

The percentage of the public works budget spent on labour wages has remained high since the start of VUP, in 2009/10, it was 88 percent. The remainder of the program's budget goes to inputs, supervision, and contractor costs for worksite supervision. On average, a participating household worked 69 days in 2009/10 and earned a total of RF 63,423 (US $109) in wages, equivalent to RF 454 (US $0.78) per day (Subbaro *et al* 2013). Most importantly, information collected on beneficiaries' use of their public works wage income from VUP shows they are being invested in similar ways as direct support transfers on consumption, human capital, asset accumulation, house building and renovation, income-generating activities, and savings. There was an average of one project per sector in 2008 and during the season running from January to June 2009, and two projects per sector in 2009/10 (123 in total for the year). Environmental protection projects (mainly anti-erosion ditches and terraces) have predominated and continue to increase in number.

More so, such projects accounted for 58 percent of the works undertaken in 2008 and 72 percent of those undertaken in 2009/10. Roads are the second most common type of VUP public works project. Project types have diversified over time. New projects implemented in 2009/10 included the construction of school classrooms, marketplaces, water infrastructure, health centres, improved furnaces, bridges, and crop cultivation (Government of Rwanda 2007; World Bank 2010). The VUP public works component, like most of Rwanda's programs initiated since 2000, relies on decentralised implementation. Much of the administration and implementation of Rwandan programmes occurs at the district, sector, cell, and village levels. The Ministry of Local Government (MINALOC) oversees the activities of these decentralised entities. It is also the ministry responsible for VUP oversight and monitoring. During VUP public works program design, the following key pillars of wage setting were identified: First, wages should be set locally (at the sector level), not nationally. Second, wages should be set as less than or equal to market rates for similar work, and include a requirement of 8 hours of work per day. Third, wages should be set on a project-by-project basis according to project type. Much of the motivation for these pillars stems from previous experiences, which have provided insight on the practical operational support requirements to turn design features into workable programme arrangements.

Successes and possible shortfalls of PWPs in Rwanda

PWPs have played an important role in bridging the gap between the poor and the rich in Rwanda. This is because of the advantages that come with the implementation of PWPS. PWPs often adopts self-targeting approach where the wage rates are lower than those prevailing in agricultural/casual wage labour so that only the poorest would be willing to accept such offer (Slater & Farrington, 2010). The lower wage makes PWPs a cheaper social protection option. Surrender (2010) argues that the provision of social protection in the form of employment through PWPs in Rwanda reduces dependency syndrome unlike cash transfer. Furthermore, PWPs promote the use and management of locally available human and material resources for the construction and maintenance of infrastructure. A well designed public works can help create vital physical infrastructure which are usually lacking in developing countries thereby boosting productivity and reducing transaction cost (OECD, 2006).

Nevertheless, despite their advantages, PWPs in Rwanda have bad reputation for some reasons. They interrupt poor households' usual livelihood activities and are not always well-targeted. Scarcity of resources requires proper targeting to ensure their efficient utilisation especially in developing countries (Slater & Farrington, 2010). However, due to flaws in design and implementation, PWPs often fails to reach the very poor. These targeting challenges are reported in a number of studies conducted on PWPs in Africa.

Rosas and Sabarwal (2014) identified major errors of inclusion and exclusion as many beneficiaries of the cash for work programme belonged to the upper quintiles indicating that the programme was not well-targeted to poor households. Adato and Haddad (2002) also identified similar weakness in targeting of PWPs for social protection in the country as they conclude that there is little evidence of the targeting of PWPs to the poorest among the poor.

Similarly, evidence on whether infrastructural assets created through PWPs last for a longer period and actually contributes in the reduction of chronic poverty remains scanty. In a study on the impact of public works on livelihood of poor households in Africa, McCord and Farrington (2008), found that through PWPs, some productive assets are created but there is little empirical evidence that these assets have any positive livelihood impact among the poor. The study identified consumption smoothing as the main benefit of PWPs but advocates the need for more and better empirical studies to justify the huge sums of money spent by governments and donor agencies on these projects. Robinson and Torvik (2005) indicates that benefits from assets created through public works may be limited because of low quality, poor integration with national infrastructure systems and lack of resources for maintenance and repair.

Lessons Learned and Conclusions

Rwanda's PWPs have evolved over time, drawing on earlier programmes and refining policy and implementation arrangements along the way. Under VUP, MINALOC continues to seek new ways to draw lessons from challenges that have arisen during the course of implementation. For each new phase of the VUP scale-up plan, MINALOC, with assistance from its development partners, has reviewed and reassessed the programme to ensure better delivery of cash transfers consistent with best international practice and overall VUP policy objectives. The key lessons of the VUP public works programme are as follow:

- Implementing a policy of clear and coordinated communication ensures the delivery of consistent messages to local officials and beneficiaries; this in turn leads to consistent practices across participating sectors and avoids or at least reduces confusion and the potential for discrediting the public works programme's long-term objectives.

- Effective communication also ensures that the benefits of setting wages for public works in accordance with international practice as has been achieved under VUP over time and that this is clearly understood by beneficiary communities as well as by eligible households.

- Geographic and seasonal variations in Rwanda's market wage rates make local wage setting a sensible approach, even though there is value in setting local wages within a coordinated national framework.

- By setting wages at or close to market rates for each project, VUP objectives are supported in terms of helping households save, invest, be able to access credit, and graduate from the program.

- Monitoring processes are critical but need continued refinement in light of initial experiences. In addition, systematic assessment of administrative interactions among government levels and the development of action plans to address related challenges could further increase the efficiency of program implementation (World Bank 2011).

Nature and scope of PWPs in Zimbabwe

In Zimbabwe the term Public Works (PWPs) has become increasingly associated with community level efforts to generate assets and at the same time help people to copy through and with the impact of drought. According to Samson and others (2006), PWPs refers to the regular payment of money or in kind benefits by government or NGOs to individuals in exchange for work aiming to decrease chronic poverty or that kind of poverty which is normally caused by a shock by providing social protection as well as taking note of social risky or reduce economic vulnerability.

Zimbabwe has a long history and experience with PWPs to fight against chronic poverty and address unemployment during periods of economic crisis. Above all, in Zimbabwe PWPs have been undertaken as part of government job creation efforts and as a poverty alleviation measure as from 1984. It is important to note that the training aspect and assumption that it will enable beneficiaries to find employment at the end of the life span of PWPs are pivotal to the implementation of PWPs as a strategy of poverty alleviation. PWPs have become a vital facet to deliver humanitarian assistance in post disaster, post conflict situations or slack agricultural seasons.

The primary rationale of PWPs is that of poverty alleviation through labour absorption. McCord (2002) opines that governments achieve the objective of poverty alleviation by spending money on the generation of public assets through labour intensive methods. The Overseas Development Institute (2012) notes that PWPs are expected to reduce reliance on social protection and contribute to economic growth as well as poverty alleviation. This is what makes them an alternative policy option for the government of Zimbabwe.

Howell (2003) notes that, the success of PWPs world over depends on their design features, and the implementation aspect. It is interesting to note that this assertion is similar to that of McCord (2003) who pointed out that the achievements of the objectives of PWPs depend largely on programme design, institutional capacity for implementation and the addition of social development considerations to public works projects that are undertaken and implemented. Besides, Queen *et al* (2006) argue that PWPs which aim to address chronic poverty should also provide a chance for beneficiaries save and accumulate assets and permit these beneficiaries to take part in other government initiatives such as training for permanent employment and establishing income generating activities.

In Zimbabwe public works has often been associated with capital intensive construction projects in the country (Karenga 2009). These may include government buildings, hospitals, universities and small labour intensive efforts at community level like road maintenance, gulley reclamation, water point rehabilitation and so on. However, the term public works has been increasingly associated with community level efforts to build assets and help people to cope with the impact of drought. It is important to note that participation in the works is intended to be self-targeted with needy homesteads presenting themselves for work at any given time.

For Karenga (1996), a public works register is kept locally. There are two distinct categories which are free public assistance and public works assistance. It is important to point out that, those individual households with young men and women participate in actual activities whilst those without can receive the same remittance for free. This helps to harmonise social assistance funding streams from head office down to the grassroots. Nevertheless, it is sad to note that targeting is very unfair and is driven by overambitious councillors and community leaders with limited knowledge on programme outcomes and benefits.

The public works policy is designed by the central government and imposed upon the local authorities to execute. The question remains, Can rural poverty be successfully alleviated using ideas that are made without the input of the intended beneficiaries. The idea interrogated the benefits brought by public works in relation to the people's basic needs. The question is that do the people really welcome some of the projects that are brought in by public works. It can be argued that an interventionist strategy such as public works conceived in the mind set of modernisation to alleviate poverty should be suspected of reinforcing the institution through the creation of the dependency syndrome.

In 1991, Zimbabwe joined a growing community of developing countries which implemented the IMF/World Bank structural adjustment programmes in an attempt to revamp their ailing economies (Mlambo 1992). Zimbabwe turned to these multilateral lending agencies because she found herself facing balance of payment problems partly as a result of flawed economic policies in the past and external forces beyond her control. The adoption of ESAP reveals that there is an ambiguous relation in Zimbabwe's development policies.

The public works intervention policy speaks the same language with ESAP that is agitating for the reduction of budget deficit, as well as removing government subsidies on goods and services. It is important to point out that ESAP is more hostile to public works owing to the fact that they dig deeper into the pockets of the government. According to Moyo *et al* (2014), the fate of public works after the adoption of ESAP in 1991 hung precariously in the balance. Theoretically, after 1991 there was supposed to be no public works since ESAP stressed on the total disengagement of government from providing social service as well as public investment. Although the government continues to have the Ministry of Public Works which administer some projects aimed at poverty alleviation in rural and urban centres, Matunhu (2009) asserts that poverty is predominantly a rural phenomenon.

The Government of Zimbabwe in 2003 enacted a new statutory instrument which regulated the operations of NGOs. The policy on NGOs in humanitarian and development assistance stressed the need to integrate public works in humanitarian assistance (Moyo *et al* 2014). It stresses that no aid for the poor was to come as social welfare but people should be given development projects targeted at the construction of infrastructure as well as enhancing their lives through public works (Government of Zimbabwe, July 2003).

Interestingly, the Zimbabwean experiences with PWPs tries to draw attention to the idea that if poverty is a socially constructed phenomenon as suggested by the structural dependency theory, then why not look back at the society for its deconstruction. A question that remains unanswered is that can rural poverty be successfully reduced using programmes that are made without the input of the intended beneficiaries?

PWPs approaches in Zimbabwe have moved from reactionary strategies aimed at mitigating drought and dependency in the early 1980s to more integrated humanitarian efforts by both the state and non-state sector in 2009. In addition to that, payment in cash or kind has largely addressed immediate or short term needs of the poor and vulnerable communities in rural Zimbabwe. Karenga (2009) stresses that the assets created or rehabilitated have longer term merits for those people who earn low salaries, in terms of livelihood viability coping. It can be noted that community based PWPs through state and non-state actors have introduced formalised element of protection by providing relief from deprivation during drought and other shocks in the form of cash and food transfers and promotion by enhancing incomes through useful public assets.

Inclusion and exclusion

Moyo *et al* (2014) argue that social exclusion is the inability of people to take part fully in any social, political and economic functioning of the society. With this, it is very important for people to have a chance to participate fully in the life of their locality if they are to flourish and realise their potential. This study found out that the effects of inclusion and exclusion in targeted PWPs vary depending on the implementation of the programme. In Zimbabwe, the people use the system of rotation rather than targeting. The rotation system is where different homesteads benefit from participation in public works projects each month with the objective of reaching as many households as possible with income transfer. With this, it can be noted that, the rotation system works against targeting the transfers to households with needy and providing them with a significant number of transfers so as to attain a substantive seasonal impact on their situations.

Contribution of PWPs in poverty alleviation

PWPs in Zimbabwe are such a relief necessary given the poverty situation in the country. However, the situation of the beneficiaries of these PWPs is normally temporarily reversed by earning a wage for the period stipulated. PWPs are of great significance to rural dwellers despite their shortfalls. It is important to note that many people in rural Zimbabwe rely on PWPs for both household income and household food security.

In view of the above, we note that PWPs are useful as a poverty alleviation strategy. They increase household food security as well as cash flow. Cash flow would allow the beneficiaries to spend their incomes on buying food and other basic needs. It would also allow young men and women who reside in the rural areas to be gainfully employed.

Nevertheless, although PWPs acted as a bridge to unemployment, the scale was too low as compared to the levels of unemployment in the country which is above 80%. In addition to that, PWPs left out a lot of poor people who were without the means of securing their basic needs owing to the fact that the number of people needed for the work was limited. Although rotating participants covered this up, it only worked to a limited extent in assisting the poor. PWPs provide seasonal and temporary employment. This entails that rural dwellers will return to poverty during the periods when PWPs are not operational. Thus, PWPs fail to produce permanent employment. Generally speaking, people in Zimbabwe are against the idea that the normal food payments are packets of maize meal, beans and at times cooking oil. These people are left with no other income generating projects to get essentials like sugar, salt and so on. Against this background, it is logical to conclude that food payments has been criticised for a lack of diversity in food stuffs.

Beneficiaries of PWPs in Zimbabwe normally complain that where food is used as stipend, it takes a very long time to be given to them; hence people suffer from acute food shortages. In addition, another disadvantage of PWPs which the respondents cited was the inability of projects to continue after the end of major programmes. Insufficient monitoring and evaluation also jeopardise the sustainability of projects.

Beneficiary's perception and attitudes on public works projects and their impact

In Zimbabwe, people generally view the activities taking place as a result of PWPs as a means to an end. Not only that, they again viewed public works schemes as a life saver owing to the fact that those who worked on them were able to get a form of income and invaluable skills and information throughout the life span of projects which would be useful elsewhere. Nevertheless, these perceptions differ with individuals and from place to place.

In our field visit in the rural communities of Zimbabwe in general and Bikita district in particular we enquired about the biographical information of the beneficiaries of PWPs. Under the biographical information, the gender, age, position in the household, marital status and the level of education of the beneficiaries of PWPs was analysed. The principal reason for taking note of the age of respondents was to find out what age group is more likely to benefit from PWPs in the rural communities of Zimbabwe. In addition, the reason for probing the level of education was to investigate the beneficiaries' level of education. This is because according to information which was obtained from the review of related literature, the level of education of most beneficiaries of PWPs is very low and they have no skill what so ever to contribute to the economic growth of the nation. Most importantly, the major reason of again probing for the position of the respondents in the household was to determine the actual number of breadwinners or household heads were likely to benefit from PWPs in rural Zimbabwe. Moreover, the position of respondents in the household would help to determine what impact PWPs would have on the improvement of livelihood of their families.

Gender

One of the current issues concerning poverty alleviation is the extent to which these are able to reach and benefit women. Owing to the structure of "gender relations in our communities and the social as well as cultural and economic challenges confronting women and/or the existing biases (favouring men) in most of the programmes of development" (Dejardin 1996: 4).

However, information gathered during the field visits actually point out that the reverse is equally true. In terms of gender, out of the 25 respondents interviewed, 40% (equivalent of 10 respondents) are males whilst 60% (equivalent of 15 respondents) are females. Thus the majority of female respondents in the research gave an impression to the investigators that the majority of beneficiaries in PWPs are women. The findings indicate that the highest percentage of beneficiaries of PWPs were essentially single parents and females. This gives an impression that the majority of men are or might not be at all involved in poverty alleviation attempts. The study concludes that PWPs in rural Zimbabwe emancipated the position of women. The provision of income earning opportunities to women was believed to provide many benefits to household welfare, over and above the benefits that would be derived from giving women an equal opportunity.

Fig 4 (a) below is a pie chart to show the distribution of this by gender

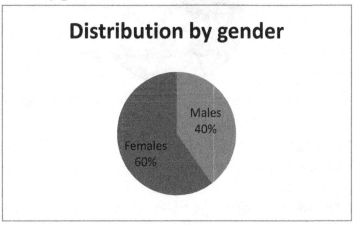

Fig 4 (a)
Source: Field Research, April 2015

4. (b) Age

In terms of the age of respondents, out of the 25 interviewed beneficiaries of PWPs in Bikita district of Zimbabwe, 8% (equivalent of 2 respondents) of the respondents are below the 18 years old. Besides, 28% (equivalent of 7 respondents) are between 18-25 years old. It can again be noted that 32% (equivalent of 8 respondents) are between 25-30 years and 52% (equivalent of 13 respondents) are above 30 years. The pie chart below shows the distribution of PWPs respondents by age.

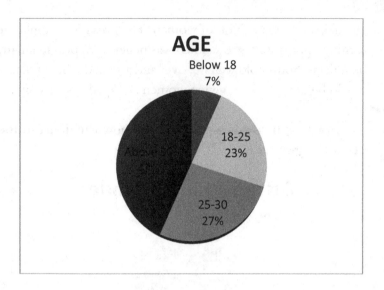

Fig 4.2.4
Source: Field Research, April 2015

According to the study, those who are below 30 years benefit most from the PWPs in Bikita district. They are followed by those between the age of 25 – 30 and those between 18 – 25 and lastly those below 18, who constitute below 7%.

4. (c) Position in the household

It can be noted that, below is a household variable result shown in table 1 and depicted in table 4. (c)

	Frequency	Percentage	Valid percentage
Head	5	20%	20
Wife/husband	8	32%	32
Son/daughter	10	40%	40
Extended family	2	8%	8%
Total	25	100	100

Table 4. (c)

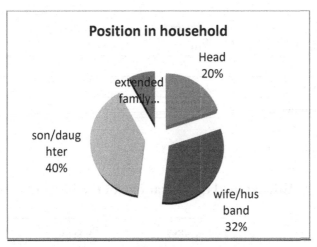

Source: Field Research, April 2015

From the diagram above, it can be noted that of the 25 households sampled in the study, 20% (equivalent of 5 respondents) represent the heads of the households who are participating in the public works programmes operational in the ward. Besides, 40% (equivalent of 10 households) represent the son and daughter. It can again be deduced that 32% (equivalent of 8 respondents) has been taken to represent the wife or the husband. Lastly, only 8% (equivalent of 2 respondents) come from the extended family.

4. (d) Marital of the respondents

In terms of the marital status of the 25 respondents, 32% (equivalent of 8 respondents) were married, 40% (equivalent of 10 respondents) were single, 12% (equivalent of 3 respondents) were divorced and 16% (equivalent of 4 respondents) were widowed. Table 4.2.6.1 below illustrate the distribution.

	Frequency	Percentages
Single	10	40
Married	8	32
Divorced	3	12
Widowed	4	16

Table 4. (d)
Source: Field Research, April 2015

4. (e) Educational qualifications of the interviewees

Educational qualifications	Frequency	Percentage
Never went to school	3	12
Primary	7	28
Secondary	10	40
Other	5	20

Table 4. (e) Source: Field Research, April 2015

The above table shows that 12% (equivalent of 3 interviewees) never went to school, 28% (equivalent of 7 interviewees) had attained primary education, 40% (equivalent of 10 interviewees) had gone through the secondary education and 20% (equivalent of 5 interviewees) had gone above secondary education. Secondary level graduates had the highest number of responses indicative of their desire to take part in PWPs in rural Zimbabwe.

4. (f) Employment status of the respondents

During the FGDs, the respondents cited the issue of unemployment as the major reason behind their participating in PWPs. The research again established that those who regarded themselves as self-employed were involved in agriculture related work, for example, processing cooking oil as well peanut butter and growing vegetables. Others were involved in piggery as well as keeping broilers. Table 4. (f) below shows the employment status of the interviewees.

Table 4. (f) Employment status of respondents

	Frequency	Percentage
In school	0	0
Unemployed	15	60
Employed temporarily	4	16
Self employed	6	24
Permanently employed	0	0

Source: *Field Research, April 2015*

The 25 respondents sampled in this research were asked to reveal their employment status. 60% (equivalent of 15 respondents) were unemployed, 16% (equivalent of 4 respondents) were employed temporarily, and 24% (equivalent of 6 respondents) were self-employed. It can be observed that the unemployed seemed to have more time at their disposal to participate in community programmes such as PWPs.

4. (g) Ownership of Assets

Of the 25 respondents sampled in this research, it can be noted that 60% (equivalent of 15 respondents) stated that they have pieces of land. Of these, 40% are males and 20% are females. Despite being culturally and economically marginalised when it comes to having land, one can note that women in rural Zimbabwe in general Bikita District in particular are finding their way to property rights. Besides, it was found that 40% of the respondents did not have pieces of land, where 18% were females and 22% were males. Non–land owners were mainly rural dwellers staying with parents and relatives. According to Jaynet *et al* (2001), Land is a very important form of social capital owing to the fact that it can sustain income growth. In addition to that, it can also aid in poverty alleviation. Fig 4.2.9.3 below summarises land ownership by gender.

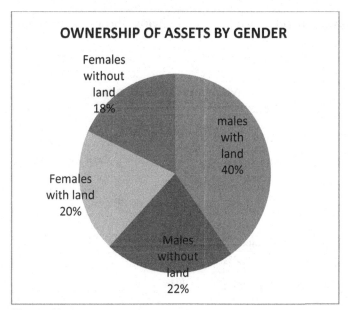

Fig 4. (g)
Source: *Field Research, April 2015*

4. Main sources of income

Multiple sources of income do exist in rural Zimbabwe in general especially Bikita district. It was found that out of the 25 households sampled in this research, 44% (equivalent of 11 households) relied on cash for work, 28% (equivalent of 7 households) relied on income from their partners. It is also important to note that 16% (equivalent of 4 households) used their own salary. In addition to that, 12% (equivalent of 3 households) responded that they used other sources. It was observed those who said they used their own salary sell fruits, mushroom, agricultural products and some insects they call *harurwa* at their nearest market which is at Nyika growth point. The majority of the respondents rely on PWPs as their source of income; hence PWPs contribute significantly to poverty alleviation in the ward. Fig 4. (h) below shows the respondents' source of income.

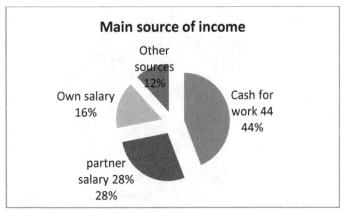

Main source of income

Other sources 12%

Own salary 16%

Cash for work 44 44%

partner salary 28% 28%

Source: *Field research, April 2015*

4. (j) Source of food

It was a finding of this research that people in ward 14 have numerous sources of food. Of the 25 sampled households, 44% (equivalent of 11 households) rely on food for work that is food handouts from public works programmes. They rely on both food and cash from PWPs to secure their food daily needs. Be that as it may, 24% (equivalent of 6 households) rely on income transfers from partner's salary, 20% (equivalent of 5 households) use salaries from temporary employment and 12% (equivalent of 3 households) said they use other sources. With this distribution, it can be safely concluded that PWPs play a major role in poverty alleviation in rural Zimbabwe. Table 4. (j) below shows the main sources of food for the respondents in the rural communities of Zimbabwe.

	Frequency	Percentage
Food for work	11	44
Cash from spouses	6	24
Salaries from temporary employment	5	20
Other sources	3	12

Table 4. (j) Source: Field Research, April 2015

The perception of poverty by the beneficiaries

The definitions of poverty which were given by respondents in rural Zimbabwe vary from one respondent to the other, showing that poverty is a multifaceted phenomenon. It was a finding of this study that most of definitions given by the respondents were comparing income and available resources in relation to their ability to meet their basic needs as well as to sustain them. The majority of the people in the ward emphasised lack of potential to meet basic necessities. These include requirements such as food as well as shelter, clothes and educational facilities. The following definitions were given:

➤ *Poverty can be defined as lack of food, clothing, shelter and health and exploitation by the elite.*

➤ *Poverty refers to a state of failing to get basic needs such as food, clothes as well as health security.*

➤ *Poverty can be defined as a pathetic state when households can no longer afford basic daily meal and when children are supposed to be in school and they are not in school owing to failure to afford paying their school fees.*

➤ *Poverty is a situation where by an individual cannot afford to meet the basic needs of life such as food, clothes and shelter after getting paid.*

➤ *Poverty can be regarded as a situation where one is in a position of failing to support him / her, even when they have the potential to do so but owing to circumstances beyond their control, they cannot.*

➤ *Poverty as you know refers to hunger and starvation, whereby an individual does not have anything to cover the body.*

➤ *Poverty can best be defined as a situation whereby one cannot afford to live an average life owing to lack of resources to cater for his family.*

➤ *Poverty can be regarded as a state of hunger and of being financially overstretched (Fieldwork Research, April 2015).*

All the above explanations and definitions of poverty point to the multifaceted nature of poverty. One can easily conclude that, poverty is best understood from people's experiences and one cannot give a one size fit all definition.

Basing on the field data from the rural communities of Zimbabwe, in cases where PWPs are implemented procedurally, beneficiaries are satisfied and were now able to do things they could not previously do. Thus beneficiaries at grassroots were able to attest to the real benefits of products delivered to them through the PWPs. However, where the policy governing the implementation of PWPs was violated or not implemented wisely, it precipitated scenarios where beneficiaries are having some negative attitudes and perceptions towards PWPs.

Generally, people feel that they were just being exploited owing to the fact that sometimes cash/grain was often not available to pay them at the end of the month upon labour provision, a development that has occurred frequently in recent years. Owing to this, it can be argued that taking part in the PWPs has decreased owing to lack of interest, poor remuneration and the selection of beneficiaries by local authorities. Moreover, young people are not inclined to join the state led PWPs as they have larger ambitions. Problems often occur at ward level where the councillor belonged to the ruling ZANU PF and beneficiaries were selected on partisan basis.

Karenga (2009) argues that placing the responsibility of beneficiary selection with the local government through its councillors, ward coordinators and VIDCO chairpersons has politicised targeting and led to the exclusion of individuals or households outside of close socio-political networks. Women, older persons and the disabled either as individuals or their representative groups are generally not involved during the planning or decision making stages. Consultation according to a number of scholars is a critical part of social assistance.

The social and economic benefits of PWPs to beneficiaries

Beneficiaries of PWPs in Zimbabwe are able to participate actively in the local economy. Their social and economic status improve due to employment generated as a result of PWPs. Besides, PWPs have helped the poor people in the country to acquire new skills and ideas with regard to economic opportunities for instance how to improve selling of their agricultural products and access to markets for their products. Of great importance is the fact that beneficiaries are receiving a stipend which enables them to join community investment clubs to help one another pay for funeral expenses in the event of death of a relative under social capital.

Effectiveness of PWPs in developing skills of the beneficiaries

PWPs have proven to be the most ideal strategy in developing skills for instance with regard to carrying out the mandate of job creation and correctly reporting jobs through a validation process that is being practiced. On top of that, the beneficiaries are given the opportunity of training at the full expense of the programme for example building, tree planting, and carpentry. PWPs are also helping future leaders to compete in an open business environment and render them skills of business acumen. PWPs have also fostered the readiness of participants to face life after the life span of PWPs has elapsed. It can also be noted that as the projects end, they will be able to use the skills they could have gained from PWPs elsewhere.

There is a positive impact of PWPs on poverty alleviation in Zimbabwe. Although poverty is still dominant in the country, it has to some extend reduced since the introduction of PWPs. It is important to note that poor people such as youth and women have benefitted from the projects through employment creation as well as monthly income. The study again revealed that women benefitted more in public works projects; this has been hailed owing to the fact that it promotes a culture of gender sensitivity.

PWPs have succeeded in uniting rural dwellers in the country in working together as a group (participatory approach), sharing thoughts, earning income and being able to secure their basic needs such as food, shelter, clothes and so on. Besides, the development of infrastructure such as road networks as well as environmental rehabilitation and construction of water sources have helped in reducing the daily hardships faced by the ward at large. The social and economic conditions and sustainable livelihoods of the poor have improved significantly.

Nevertheless, it can also be noted that year round projects have created problems in as much as it clashed with normal activities of the community for instance the summer agricultural season. Thus tension is created between jobs offered under public works and the need for labour for regular farming activities. The potential conflict between PWPs and normal economic activity should be addressed preferably by adjusting the wage rate according to seasons. In addition, despite the improved standard of living and poverty alleviation at the local level, there are still challenges as many young people are still without jobs.

From the researchers' observations, PWPs have not sufficiently reduced poverty in the country as the beneficiaries spend much of their valuable time on poorly paying jobs that consumes time. Besides, no long term employment has been generated and no effort towards this has been exerted. PWPs have short-lived the expectations of the beneficiaries owing to their short duration. People in Zimbabwe remain poor owing to the fact that they are technically handicapped and PWPs do little to emancipate them. Poverty continues to haunt people in the owing to the fact that PWPs aims at curing symptoms of poverty and there are no solid measures to ensure the sustainability of assets created by PWPs.

Conclusion

This chapter has demonstrated how PWPs can help to bridge the gap between the poor and the rich. Drawing examples from African countries in general and Rwanda, Tanzania and Zimbabwe in particular, PWPs have contributed to poverty alleviation through providing work opportunities to economically active people who are either unemployed or underemployed. PWPs have contributed to poverty alleviation in numerous ways, the most direct routes being through transferring income (in cash or in kind), and by creating useful economic infrastructure. Indirect or 'second round' effects include income multipliers generated by spending of public works wages, impacts on labour markets, and enhanced employability of workers after the programme finishes. However, the contribution of PWPs towards reducing vulnerability of households to the problems of food deprivation, unemployment and social exclusion have not produced the desired outcomes. Although many countries in Africa including Rwanda, Zimbabwe and Tanzania adopted PWPs to address poverty through cash benefits, food handouts and the creation of infrastructure that can spearhead development as a simulation from the rest of the world, the programmes had their own limitations and as such have not improved, as desired, the situation of poor people in the rural communities. Hence, the rural poor in Africa still grapple with the challenges of poverty and the efficacy of PWPs as a remedy to their poverty predicament.

Chapter 5

Public Works Programmes and Sustainable Development in Africa

Introduction

In order to fully understand the concept of sustainable development, there is need to make a clear distinction between "sustainable" and "development". To "sustain", from its earliest understanding, means "to support, to uphold the course of or keeping into being". O'Conner as with Pezzoli (1996: 6) argues that, this concept is widened to mean "to provide with food and drink or the necessities of life." Sustainability is more and more becoming a measure or an indicator of sustainable development as well as a philosophy following the principles of sustainable development. The concept "development" on its part, embraces continuous change and evolution in a variety of aspects in human society. Sustainable development concept is sometimes described as a political project aimed at developing an integrated decision-making process, which is capable of balancing economic and social needs of the people with the regenerative capacity of the environment. PWPs if properly manage can lead to sustainable development.

Understanding sustainable development in the context of Public Works Programmes

Sustainable development has never been an easy concept to define. For this reason, it has enjoyed a plethora of interpretations. Sangiga *et al* (2010), for instance, observe that sustainable development should be based on local-level solutions derived from community initiatives and should be closed to an "environmental entitlements" enabling poor people to have access on natural resources and use them in order to produce environmental services necessary for their livelihood. For development to be sustainable it requires the active involvement of people – the beneficiaries themselves – in the design and implementation of activities intended to improve their welfare. The empowerment of people to take increasing charge of their own development is the key element, combined with a clear understanding of environmental constraints and of requirements to meet basic needs (Haines, 2000). This shows that there is a close correlation between PWPs and sustainable development. For development goals to embrace the values and norms of a specific community, the members of that community have to own the decision making process. People must be central in the whole development process. They must be involved in a transformative process not just being where they are moving forward towards a future that they want. It is believed that poverty can only be removed by the substantial empowerment of people, individually and in groupings.

Several scholars agree on the fact that sustainable development should embed three main aspects: economic, social and environmental, all of them followed or preceded by the term "sustainable". Thus, sustainable development is the development approach that most countries now agree on. It deals with suing the world's resources to improve people's lives without compromising the ability of future generations to do the same.

The United Nations (1987) came up with a widely accepted definition of sustainable development. It states that sustainable development is that type of development with the potential to meet current needs without compromising the ability of future generations to meet their own needs. This means that sustainable development is futuristic besides being concerned with the present. The United Nations' definition of sustainable development also entail that sustainable development may relate to linking what is to be sustained and developed. It is from this understanding that scholars like Kates (2005) notes that another way of defining sustainable development is by its goal, that is, what it endeavours to achieve. The pillars of sustainable development according to the United Nations (1987) are economic, social, and environmental sustainable development. To this list of pillars, we add the 'political' pillar which we think is critical in providing compass or direction to development. In fact, our experience as African researchers and scholars have shown us that politics influence almost all spheres of life including the economy, culture, religion and the environment.

Parallels between Public Works Programmes and Sustainable Development Goals (SDG)

The Sustainable Development Goals (SDGs), otherwise known as the Global Goals, are a universal call to action to end poverty, protect the planet and ensure that all people enjoy peace and prosperity. These SDGs) were born at the United Nations Conference on Sustainable Development in Rio de Janeiro in 2012. The objective was to produce a set of universal goals that meet the urgent environmental, political and economic challenges facing our world.

From this understanding, there is no doubt that PWPs in Africa contribute to sustainable development. All PWPs combine three core dimensions of developmental impact which contribute to Sustainable Livelihoods. These include the impacts of the income earned, the impacts of the participation in work and the impacts of the assets and services created. Most importantly, a fourth dimension of PWPs is derived from the fact that they are also embedded in social processes. The nature as well as quality of these processes can enhance impacts on community development and build local institutions vital to wider development processes. Participation in work (whether this is market-based or not, or remunerated or not) plays a crucial social role at a wide range of levels.

Development practitioners have also noted that participation in PWPs can be associated with, increased social inclusion, a reduction in anti-social behaviour and the development of a wide range of capabilities from skills learned on the job (such as team-work, task allocation and task-management) through to more formal skills development undertaken within the work context. By enabling participation in work, PWPs contributes to these important social and economic impacts. Crucial to PWPs is the ability to provide pathways into employment is its reputation for the quality of outcomes delivered, and the productivity and efficiency of its work streams. PWPs create assets and services that contribute to the public good. Assets and services provided through PWPs significantly contributes to public investment in community infrastructure and social services, and augment the social wage in important ways. This has a massive impact on both social and economic development, contributing to the country's strategic development and creating economic value that exceeds the cost of the programme. PWPs is a source of economic value. Though not all programmes create economic value that is measurable, such programmes create social value that enhance livelihoods and strengthen social inclusion.

The sustainable development framework can be applied to PWPs in Africa as shown below. Using the sustainable development framework to look at PWPs in Africa moves it from an emphasis on political and donor cycles towards long term investment that will benefit the underdeveloped and marginalised communities in rural Africa. The framework shown below places poor rural people and their areas at the centre and show the correct pro-poor individual poor house agenda for successful outcomes.

The sustainable development framework

The sustainable development framework was adopted by world leaders in September 2015 at a historic United Nations Summit and underpinned by 17 Sustainable Development Goals (SDGs). The SDGs are expected to guide governments as they work to address some of the most pressing challenges facing humanity. The SDGs were developed following the United Nations Conference on Sustainable Development in Rio de Janeiro in 2012 and build on the Millennium Development Goals (MDGs) adopted in September 2000 as part of the un Millennium Declaration. The SDGs provide a more holistic and integrated approach to development than the MDGs. They are designed to be universal and therefore apply to all countries – poor, rich and middle-income alike – and to all segments of society. Although each focuses on a different topic area, the SDGs are meant to be integrated, indivisible and collectively support a development agenda balancing the economic, social and environmental dimensions of sustainability. While not legally binding, the SDGs do provide a globally endorsed normative framework for development. Governments and other stakeholders are expected to establish national and regional plans for their implementation. It is worth mentioning that the sustainable development framework can be applied to PWPs, for example in Zimbabwe as shown below:

A Sustainable Development Framework for PWPS in Zimbabwe

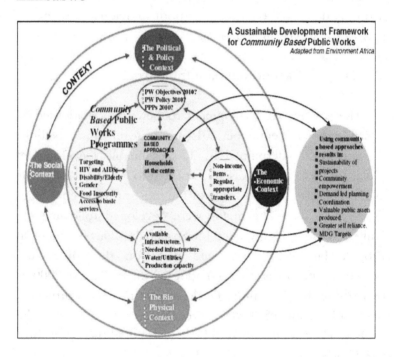

Source: Karenga (2009:12)

From the given sustainable development framework, the following conclusions can be drawn: First, the policy environment for PWs is very weak and offers little capacity or guidance for coordination. It can also be deduced that without a clear policy, co-ordination and strong political will from the elite for reforming public works programming, the economic context is weakened. The government avails resources every year, but little impact has been made and documented. The local community structures are not yet empowered within this programme (RUWP Manual, 2004). Moreover, the categorisation of PWPs by type and according to the objectives can help to see good approaches within the influencing context and allow different programmatic objectives. Besides, the changing social context should influence both the programme objectives and its strategy for support, for example, targeting is quite prominent. It is important to note that self-targeting strategies do not work effectively when the competition is high for little resources nor does it work in political structures.

The bio-physical context relates to what the majority of the poor people in rural Zimbabwe and most vulnerable individual households rely on for their living. Quality and effective social safety nets need good access to basic services and the capacity to cope with shocks in both short and long-term. Karenga (2009) argues that focusing on intermittent income transfer leaves communities poor. Thus, it is logical to argue that enhanced livelihood systems are therefore imperative for Africa's many communal farms and regular and decent work opportunities are needed for the country's unemployed.

Basing on the case studies of Tanzania, Rwanda and Zimbabwe, PWPs can help to promote sustainable development in a number of ways. In these countries, many people rely on PWPs for both household incomes as well as sources of food. Most importantly, PWPs are useful as a move towards poverty alleviation as they increase household food security as well as cash inflow. The latter would allow beneficiaries to spend their incomes on any combination food and other necessities of their choice. In the event, the cash-for-work scheme would guarantee minimum income to the most vulnerable while encouraging able-bodied individuals to be gainfully employed. It would also maintain the incentive to work and would eliminate the tendency to be continually aid dependent. In Zimbabwe, for instance, for the majority of beneficiary households the money went towards the purchase of household items such as salt, soap, clothes and other foodstuff such as cooking oil and dried fish (the latter leading to a diversification of diets). A number of households also invested in school fees for their children and the purchase of small livestock and were able to pay for health costs. Some few respondents talked about the rehabilitation of their homes.

Besides, women are generally the beneficiaries of PWPs. This helps to promote a culture of gender sensitivity. Generally, providing work for rural women in Africa has seen more benefits trickling into the households as compared to providing work for men. This is because most of the income is used for household use, which rarely occurs with most men who reduce their families to poverty by using the money on beer. The involvement and participation of women in the decision-making process has also been instrumental, as it has seen the suggestion of very useful projects. Furthermore, infrastructure like village tracks and water weirs have helped to reduce the day-to-day hardships faced by these women and their communities at large.

Conclusion

This chapter has underlined that what is understood as "sustainable development" in contemporary discourses is a matter of contention. For this reason, it has enjoyed a plethora of explanations from different scholars across disciplines. However, scholars seem to agree that sustainable development should be based on grassroots solutions derived from community initiatives to foster 'real' development. In this case, genuine sustainable development requires the active involvement of the intended beneficiaries. Thus, well managed and carefully planned PWPs can contribute to sustainable development in Africa. They contribute to employment creation, poverty alleviation and generate assets and services that can be used by future generations. Most importantly, they contribute immensely to public investment in community infrastructure and social services.

Chapter 6

Public Works Programmes that Work: A Seed for Rural Development?

"It is only public works programmes that work for the intended people which can germinate into real development for rural areas" (Munyaradzi Mawere 2017)

Introduction

Generally speaking, PWPs can contribute to poverty alleviation and sustainable development in Africa. They can play an important role in the economic development of countries especially where structural unemployment and chronic poverty are prevalent. The major findings for this book are mainly from the case studies of Zimbabwe, Rwanda and Tanzania.

From what we harvested from the aforementioned case studies, PWPs can only be successful if its design elements and implementation aspects are appropriate for responding to unemployment and poverty on a large scale. The contribution of this book should be to make recommendations for areas of improvement with regard to the design elements and implementation aspects of the infrastructure sector of the PWPs. These recommendations, based on international best practices, have been made so that the infrastructure sector of the PWPs can more effectively contribute towards curbing unemployment and poverty in Africa by making the unemployed more employable. This is vital in ensuring the improvement in the quality of life of a large proportion of

Africa's population and to ensure that its economy continues to grow sustainably and productively.

In light of the analysis given in this book, it is logical to conclude that most African governments adopted PWPs in an attempt to reduce the adverse effects of poverty in both rural and urban areas. The strategy became a prominent initiative to poverty alleviation and employment creation through labour absorption. Besides, PWPs are often used as a social protection instrument to address the needs of the working age poor. In fact PWPs are expected to reduce reliance on social protection and also contribute towards economic growth. It is important to note that PWPs lead to job creation for social protection providing a "win-win" combination of welfare transfers and the generation of useful assets. This is what makes it an attractive policy option for most governments in Africa and abroad. The whole framework governing public works programmes is formulated by the central government and delegated to local authorities to implement. The local authorities are expected to develop infrastructure in their areas of jurisdiction. Therefore, in the process, the projects are able to cushion people from the adverse effects of poverty, but most especially if people are always considered first and development later.

PWPs are very crucial as a poverty alleviation strategy owing to the fact that they increase household food security and cash inflow. They have been regarded as a life saver by the people in African countries. The respondents also stressed that the programmes have proven to be best in developing skills since beneficiaries are sometimes given an opportunity of training at the full expense of the programme. After the life span of the project they will be able to use the same skills to get employment elsewhere.

Nevertheless, whilst the PWPs were applauded for their merits, it appears there are some demerits that are inherent in them. A significant number of beneficiaries have criticised them for micro focusing in the sense that few people end up benefiting from the programme which pay little dividends. Participating in PWPs has declined as a consequence of lack of interest, poor remuneration and the selection of beneficiaries by the local authorities. In Zimbabwe, problems are occurring at ward level where a councillor belongs to the ruling ZANU-PF and beneficiaries are selected on partisan basis. Beneficiaries claimed that placing the responsibility of beneficiary identification and selection to the local government through its councillors has politicised targeting and led to a complete exclusion of individuals or households outside close social and political networks.

What needs to be done to end poverty through PWPs in rural Africa?

The recommendations in this book are based on the findings from the field, personal experiences and a body of literature reviewed and analysed. These recommendations are made to African governments which endeavour to tackle poverty through PWPs to ensure the relevant contributions of managing public works are necessitated:

- It was noted that at the delivery or grassroots level, the institutional arrangement of the programme is very weak and non-existent in most cases leading to poor governance. Against this background, it is recommended that during the design stage, institutional arrangements and mechanisms should be improved through the involvement of potential beneficiaries of the public works projects to enhance service delivery.

• Besides, it is also recommended that there is need to improve the capacity and political will to follow all the guidelines, to ensure transparency and accountability and take firm action on non-compliance. In the planning stage of public works projects, there is need to allocate administrative budget to facilitate monitoring and evaluation. It is of paramount importance for monitoring and evaluation to be done on a more regular basis. Above all, the beneficiaries of public works projects should form part of the monitoring and evaluation of the programme to solicit comments and input from the poor beneficiaries.

• Poverty summits must be organised on yearly basis to enhance programme and project planning process. Besides, the programme implementation process should involve all the stake holders and be consultative with the grassroots people to seek benefit from it.

• Gender mainstreaming must form part of the project management and programme design. This therefore means vulnerable groups of people such as women and orphans are accorded special status in the programme. PWPs should encourage women participation and this can also be done by consulting participants in the local area.

• The governments are is recommended to move away from the local government led functional units to the broad stakeholder committees informed by localised safety net planning. It was deduced that politics has polarised communities and perpetuate social exclusion across programmes.

- In addition, putting in place representative groups at grass root level can help with inclusion strategies across programmes.

- It is of great importance to build trust and understanding on PWPs through concerted communication efforts. Programming of PWPs at national level needs a sound communication, information and education plan and support, transparency and accountability through common implementation standards and expectations.

- Be that as it may, PWPs should be synchronised to the timing of agricultural slack seasons especially in the rural communities in Africa, the key challenge to this has been administrative in nature in nature with funds arriving late.

- The design of public works programme itself should address the basic needs of the people. In this context, there is need to ask communities what they want. It is quite authentic to say developing programmes with the beneficiaries ensures a regulatory structures, trust, transparency and accountability. With this, it can therefore be argued that this reinforces the need for community based planning approaches where appropriate.

- The authorities are also recommended to ensure guidance on targeting and inclusion. There is need to document and share the best practices on how communities can help each other. It was deduced that on the ground there are contradictory views on what public works are and how targeting in PWPs can be best implemented. Therefore, this means that, information will enable the rural villages to decide wisely on particular situations about public works.

- In as far as targeting of beneficiaries is concerned, it should start with the vulnerability assessment and there is need for a marked level of serious cooperation between actors than during the needs assessment and the beneficiary selection.

- There are numerous non – governmental organisations (NGOs) and donor agencies in Zimbabwe that can do a splendid job with the help of the government. It can be argued that if all efforts on PWPs are well planned and coordinated at national level, PWPs can be very effective and indeed act as a panacea to poverty alleviation.

- African governments are recommended to engage all players in the central forum to commence the coordination process. It is important to note that the prevailing uncertainty in the operational environment requires a flexible and multifaceted approach if PWPs are to realise the desired objectives.

- Furthermore, there is need for the Africa to improve guidelines on the goals, ensure transparency and accountability as well as monitoring and evaluation of PWPs activities either as a standalone programme, an integrated relief programme or a development tool.

- It is of great significance to link guidelines to district and ward level plans. Africa is therefore a requirement to agree and set objectives with associated indicators and outcomes, provision of reporting standards that include progress against indicators and a monitoring plan.

- Above all, there is also need to state in very clear terms the roles and responsibilities of different actors at each level that is central, provincial, and ministerial, district, ward and VIDCO, state and non-state as well as the harmonisation of procedures for both urban and rural programmes.

- Subbaro (2003) notes that in the designing of Public Works policy in general as well as implementation of programmes, there are six considerations that need careful and regular review which he summarises as follows:

- *That public works programmes provide income in the form of cash to those households in need of this type of assistance.*

- *PWPs should also enable households to meet any consumption/shortfalls they may encounter during slack agricultural periods depending on the timing.*

- *That well designed PWPs should construct much —needed infrastructure and endeavour to minimise the trade-off between public spending on income transfers versus public spending on developmental projects.*

- *That fixed assets that PWPs generate have the ability to create second round employment benefits as the much needed infrastructure is developed.*

- *That public works programmes can easily be targeted to specific geographical areas that are experiencing high unemployment and poverty rates.*

- *That public works programmes have helped many small private contractors to emerge and as well grow (p. 6).*

Conclusion

To conclude this book, we note that PWPs can play a significant role in the economic development of African countries, especially where structural unemployment and chronic poverty are prevalent. It is worth noting that PWPs can only be successful if its design elements and implementation aspects are appropriate for responding to unemployment and poverty on a large scale. Although poverty is still dominant in Africa, it has to some extend been reduced since the introduction of PWPs by respective governments. Poor people such as youths and women have benefitted from the projects through employment creation as well as monthly income.

Nevertheless, it can also be noted that year round projects have created problems in as much as they clash with normal activities of the community, for instance, the summer agricultural season. Thus, tension is created between jobs offered under public works programmes and the need for labour for regular farming activities. Beneficiaries of PWPs in the selected case studies recommended that the potential conflict between PWPs and normal economic activity should be addressed preferably by adjusting the wage rate according to seasons. In addition, despite the improved standard of living and poverty alleviation at the local level, there are still challenges as many young people are still without jobs.

Basing on the information harvested from the field, PWPs have not sufficiently reduced poverty in Africa the beneficiaries spend much of their valuable time on poorly paying jobs that consumes time. It was also a finding of this study that no long term employment has been generated and no effort towards this has been exerted. Thus PWPs have short-lived the expectations of the beneficiaries owing to their short duration. Poverty continues to haunt people in sub Saharan Africa owing to the fact that PWPs aims at curing symptoms of poverty and there are no solid measures to ensure the sustainability of assets created by PWPs

In Zimbabwe, it was learnt that there is too little or no training that is associated with the public works programmes, hence there is no capacity building for people to get formally employed under the programme. This was concluded to be one reason why the people in rural communities in Africa remain deprived of employment. They are technically handicapped and programmes do little to foster their needs and emancipation as a people. It can, therefore, be concluded that although public works programmes have not been significantly active at reducing some effects of poverty in sub-Saharan Africa, they were also instrumental as they brought some useful outcomes. More importantly, public works programmes can do more to alleviate or even eradicate poverty if people are prioritised before the prioritisation of development itself.

Directions for future research

Although the research which culminated into the present book on *Public Works Programmes: A strategy for poverty alleviation and rural development in sub-Saharan Africa?* was successfully carried out, there are still pockets of intellectual gaps that need to be filled such as:

❖ Those that relate to the gender dimension in public works programmes.

❖ Youth development through public works initiatives in Africa.

❖ Public works programmes as an employment creation strategy in Africa.

These areas have not been fully researched for this book as the focus was different, yet they are equally important issues as far as development in rural Africa is concerned.

References

Adaro, M. and Haddad, L. (2002) Targeting Poverty through Community-Based Public Works Programmes: Experience from South Africa, *The Journal of Development Studies*, 38(3): 1-36.

Alam, K. R. (2006) Gonokendra, An innovative model for poverty alleviation in Bangladesh, *Interview Review of Education*, 10 (52): 343-352.

Alcock, P. (1993) *Understanding Poverty*, The Macmillan Press. London.

Ahmed, R, and Hossain, M. (1990) Developmental Impact of Rural Infrastructure in Bangladesh, *BIDS Research Report 83*, Washington, D.C.: International Food Policy Research Institute in collaboration with the Bangladesh Institute of Development Studies.

Amin, S. (1972) Underdevelopment and Dependence in Black Africa: Origins of Contemporary Forms, *Journal of Modern African Studies* 1 (10): 503 -24.

Bosu, K. (1987) "The elimination of persistent hunger in South East Asia: policy options politico" in J.P. Dreze and A.K., Sen (Eds) *The political economy of hunger*, Oxford University Press, Oxford.

Burger, R., and Von F. D. (2009) Determining the cause of the rising South African employment rate: Period and Generation, *Working paper No 158*, University of Stellenbosch and University of Oxford.

Carlo, D., Subbaro, K., and Milazo, A. (2009) How to make public works work, A review of the experiences, *SP discussion papers*, Number 0905.

Chani, C. (2008) International cross border trade, *A review of its impact on house hold poverty reduction (Zimbabwe)*, A thesis submitted in partial fulfilment of the requirements of a Masters of social science degree in development studies, University of Fort Hare.

Chambers, R. (2004) Ideas for Development, *IDS Working Paper 238*, IDS: Sussex.

Chambers, R. (2006) *What is poverty? Who asks? Who answers?* In D. Ehrenpreis (Ed), Poverty in Focus, (pp. 7-9). Brasilia: UNDP International poverty centre.

Chinake, H. (1997) Strategies for poverty alleviation in Zimbabwe, *Journal for Social development in Africa*, 12 (1): 39-51.

Chikwanha-Dzenga Annie Barbara. (1999) Rural Folks - The Neglected Lot of Zimbabwe, *Journal of Social Development in Africa*, 14 (2):39-49.

Clay, E. J. (1986) Rural public works and food for work: A Survey, *World development*, 14 (10/11): 1237-1252.

Datt, G., and Ravalion, M. (1994) Transfer benefits from public works employment, evidence for rural India, *Economic journal* 104, November, 1346-1369.

De Beer, F & Swanepoel, H. (2000) *Introduction to development studies*, Cape Town: Oxford University Press.

Dercon, S. (2009) *Rural Poverty: Old Challenges in New Contexts*, Oxford University Press: Oxford.

Derjadin, A. (1996) "Public works programmes", A strategy for poverty alleviation: The gender dimension, issues in development, *Discussion Paper* 10, ILO, Geneva.

De Vos, A. S., Strydom, H., Fouche, C. B., and Deport, C. S. C. (2005) *Research at grassroots: for the social sciences and human service professions*, Pretoria, Van Schaik.

Economy Watch. (2010, October 4) *Unemployment and poverty*, Retrieved 18 April 2015, from www.economywatch.com/unemployment/poverty/html

Feuerstein, M. (1997) *Poverty and health*, Macmillan, London.

Foster, J. E. (1998) "Absolute versus relative poverty", *The American economic review vol. 88, no. 2*. Papers and preceding's of the Hundred and tenth annual meeting of the American Economic Association.

FAO. (1984) *Economic and social development 44*, economic strategies for the poor, United Nations, Washington DC.

Foster, J. (1984) A Case of Decomposable Poverty Measures, *Econometirca*, 52: 761-765

Garnier, P. (1992) Fighting poverty by promoting employment and socio- Economic rights of the grassroots, *international labour review* Vol 131(1):55-63

Gaude, J., and Watzlawick, H. (1992) Employment creation and poverty alleviation through labour intensive public works in least developed countries, *international labour review* 131(1): 3-18

Goulet, D. (1992) Participation in development: new avenues. *World Development* 17(2): 165-178.

Government of Rwanda. (2007) *Vision 2020 Umurenge Program (VUP)*. Program document, Kigali.

Government of Zimbabwe. (1994) *Poverty alleviation action plan*, Zimbabwe Government Printers, Harare.

Greenberg, A. (2005) *ICJ for poverty alleviation: basic tool and enabling sector*, SIDA.

Giraud, A. (2006) The distributive politics of emergency employment programmes in Argentina (1993-2000), *Latin American research review*, 42 (2): 33-35.

Guichard, S., and Rusticell, E. (2010 October 14) *Assessing the impact of the financial crisis in structural unemployment in OECD*

139

countries, Unemployment Developments after crisis presented at the 7th European Central Bank/ Centre for policy research labour market workshop, German, Frankfurt.

Haines, R. (2000) Development theory in F de Beer & H, Swanepol (Eds), *Introduction to development studies* (pp31-58), Oxford University Press, New York.

Hague, W. (2007) *International community has a moral responsibility to speak*, In Mail and Guardian, April 20 to 25, South Africa.

Hatla, B. R. (2010) The impact of government grants on poverty in Sharpeville, PhD Thesis, Vanderbijlpark: North West University. Hartwell R. M. 1972. *The Consequences of the Industrial Revolution in England for the Poor in the Institute of Economic Affairs, The Long Debate on Poverty*, The Unwin Brothers, Surrey.

Hettne, B. (1995) *Development Theory and the three worlds: towards an international political economy of development, (2nd Ed.)*. Longman, Harlow.

Hettne, B. (2009) *Thinking about Development*. Zed Books.

Holt, J. F. J. (1983) Ethiopia: Food for work or food for relief, *Food policy* Vol 8, NO 3, August.

Howell, F. (2001) *Strategies for improved social protection in Asia*, Philippines, Manila.

Idriss Jazaïry; Alamgir, Mohiuddin; Panuccio, Theresa. (1992) *The State of World Rural Poverty: An Inquiry into Its Causes and Consequences*. New York University Press, New York.

IFAD. (2005) *Achieving millennium development goals, rural investment and enabling policy*, United Nations, Washington DC.

Islam, R. (2001) *Poverty alleviation, employment and labour market: Lessons from the Asian experience: A paper prepared on behalf of the Asian Development Bank presented at the Asian pacific forum* on poverty, reforming policies and institutions for poverty reduction, Philippines, Manila.

Jacobs, G., and Slaus, I. (2011) Global prospects for full employment, *The camas journal* 1(2): 60-89.

Janvry, A. de, E. Sadoulet, & R. Murgai. (2002) Rural Development and Rural Policy. In B. Gardner, & G. Rausser (eds.), *Handbook of Agricultural Economics*, vol. 2, A, Amsterdam: North Holland: 1593–658.

Jayne, T. S. *et al.* (2001) *Smallholder income and land distribution in Africa, implication for poverty reduction strategies*, Michigan University, Department of agricultural economics.

Johanne, R. (2007) *The measurement of poverty in South Africa project: Key issues. Poverty and inequality institute. [Web:] http://www.the-measures-ofpoverty-in-South-Africa.html* [Date of access: 15 September 2017).

Johnson, S. (1993) *The earth summit: the United Nations Summit on environment and development*, London, Graham & Trotman.

Kapinga, D. S. (2006) Rural Development Issues; Lecture notes compendium for MARD SUA, Morogoro 18pp.Karenga, K., W.2009. *An analysis of government and NGO public works/food for work approaches in Zimbabwe*, MDTF Funded Research, Harare.

Knutsson, B. (2009) The Intellectual History of Development-towards a widening potential repertoire, *Perspectives*, 13 (1): 2-46.

Kostzer, D., Lan, R., Lieuw-Kie-Song, M. & Miller, S. (2010) *June Public works and employment programmes: Towards a long term development approach (Working paper 16) poverty group of the United Nations Development Programme and policy international*, Centre for Inclusive Growth, Washington DC.

Kothari, R. (1993) *Poverty human consciousness and the amnesia of Development*, Zed Books, London.

Kusek, J. Z. & Rist, C. R. (2004) *A handbook to development practitioners: Ten steps to a result based monitoring and evaluation system*, Washington DC, the World Bank.

Mabogunje, A. (1980) *The Development Process: A Spatial Perspective*, Hutchinson, London.

Makombe, I. A. M., Temba, E. I. & Kihombo, A. R. M. (1999) Credit schemes and Women's Empowerment for Poverty Alleviation: The case of Tanga Region, Tanzania; REPOA *Research Report No 99 (1)*. Dar es Salam, Tanzania.

Mkapa, B. W. (2004) *Statement by the President of the United Republic of Tanzania at the World Bank Conference on scaling up poverty reduction*. Shanghai International Convention Centre, Peoples Republic of China [http://wwwtanzania .gotz/hotuba] site visited on 26/5/2009.

Manamela, N. J. (1993) The 1992-93 drought in Botswana— the relief program components, process, and outcomes, *International Food Policy Research Institute*, Washington, D.C. Mimeo.

Martens, B. (1989) *Economic development that lasts: Labour-intensive irrigation projects in Nepal and the United Republic of Tanzania*, Geneva: International Labour Office.

Matunhu, J. (2011) A critique of modernisation and dependency theories in Africa, *African journal of history and culture*, 3 (5): 65-72.

Matunhu, J. (2012) The indigenisation and economic empowerment policies in Zimbabwe: opportunities and challenges for rural Development *in southern peace review journal, vol 12 (1):98-106*.

Mawere, M. (2017a) *Theorising development in Africa: Towards building an African framework of development*, Langaa Publishers: Bamenda.

Mawere, M. (2017b) The political economy of poverty and vulnerability: How Africa can break the cycle of poverty to unlock its underdevelopment jam? *Paper Presented at ASA Annual Meeting*, Washington DC, USA.

McCord, A. (2003) An overview of the performance of public works in South Africa, *Paper prepared for Drpu*, Tips forum, Johannesburg, South Africa.

McCord, A. & Farrington, J. (2008) Digging holes and filling them in again? How far do public works enhance livelihoods? Overseas Development Institute. *Natural Resource Perspectives 120*.

Mlambo, A. S. (1992) *The economic structural adjustment programme: The case of Zimbabwe*, Harare, University of Zimbabwe publications.

Moyo, L., Oluyinka, O. & Onyen, K. (2014) An assessment of public works as a poverty reduction Strategy for Rural Zimbabwe: A study on Chivi District, *Mediterranean journal of social sciences* 5 (23): 2039-2117.

Mullen, J. (1995) *Rural poverty alleviation, international development perspective*, Avebury, Aldershot.

Mvula, P. (2000) *Assessment of the public works programmes in Malawi*, Lilongwe: Wadonda publishers.

Muzaale Patrick J. (1987) Rural Poverty, Social Development and Their Implications for Fieldwork Practice. *Journal of Social Development in Africa*, 5 (2): 75-85.

Nyati, D. (2012) *An evaluation of poverty alleviation strategies by non-governmental organisations (NGOs) in Zimbabwe: A case of Binga rural district*, dissertation submitted in partial fulfilment of Master of Sciences degree in Development studies, South Africa, University of Fort Hare.

Novak, T. (1998) *Poverty and the state*, Open University Press, Milton Keynes.

Overseas development institute. (2006) *Approving productivity, enhancing PWPs, (Social protection tool sheet page 1-8)* retrieved on 20 July 2016, from overseas development institute, website:
http//www.odi.org.uk/resources/docs/7683.pdf.

Pellissery, S. (2008) Micro-politics of social protection: Examining the effectiveness of employment rights for the informal sector in rural Maharashtra, *Journal contemporary south Asia*, 16 (2): 197-215.

Pezzoli, K. (1996) *Sustainable development, a transdisciplinary overview of the literature, Urban Studies Planning*, University of California, USA.

Phillips, S. (2004) Overcoming underdevelopment in South Africa's second economy, *Paper prepared for EPWP conference jointly hosted by the UNDP, HSRC and DBSA*, National Department of Public Works, Johannesburg.

Porter, M., Stern, S. & Artavia Loría, R. (2013) *Social Progress Index 2013*, Washington D.C.: Social Progress Imperative.

Quene, K.M., Samson, M., & Van Nierkerk, S. (2006. Chapter 10) ' Designing issues for public works' in Designing and implementing social transfers programmes(pp1-17) Cape Town, South Africa: *Economic policy research place*, Accessed from www.epri.org.za, April 15 2015.

Quinn, V., M. Cotten, J. Mason, & B. N. Kgosioinis. (1988) *Crisis-proofing the economy: The response of Botswana to economic recession and drought, In: Adjustment with a human face, Vol. II.,* ed. G. A. Cornia, R. Jolly, and F. Steward, 3-27, Oxford University Press, New York.

Rajasekha, D. (2004) *Poverty alleviation strategies of NGOs*, India, Concept publishing company.

Rauch, T., Baterls, M., and Engel, A. (2001) *Regional rural development, A regional response to rural poverty*, Wiesbaden University press, Wiesbaden.

Ravallion, M. (1991) Reaching the poor through public employment, *The World Bank Observer* 6(2): 153-75.

Ravallion, M. (1991) On the coverage of public works schemes for poverty alleviation in *Journal of development economics*, Vol 1(34), 57-59.

Ravallion, M. (1999) Appraising workfare, *The World Bank Research Observer* 14(1): 31-48.

Ravallion, M., S. Chen, & P. Sangraula. (2007) New evidence on the urbanisation of global poverty, *World Bank Policy Research Paper 4199*.

Riddle, R., & Robinson, M. (2002) The impact of NGO poverty alleviation projects, *Working Paper 2002*, Overseas Development Institute, London.

Robinson, J. A. & Torvik, R. (2005) 'White elephants', *Journal of Public Economics* 89 (2-3): 197-210.

Rosas, N. & Sabarwal, S. (2014) How productive are productive safety nets? Evidence from Public Works in Sierra Leone. Conference Proceedings, 9th IZA/World Bank Conference on, *Employment and Development*, World Bank: Peru,
www.iza.org/conference_files/worldb2014/rosas_n1017 1.pdf

Saifudin, A. (2006) *NGO's perception of poverty in Bangladesh*, University of Bergen Press, Spring.

Samwel, E. C. (2004) Population, Sustained Economic Growth and Poverty Eradication in Tanzania. *Development Studies Journal* 5(2): 73-83.

Sanginga, P. C. *et al.* (2010) Natural resources management and development nexus in Africa, in: Sanginga, P. C., Ochola,

W. O. and Bekalo, I. (Eds): *Managing natural resources for development in Africa,* a resource book, University of Nairobi Press, Nairobi.

Save the children U. K. (2003) *Report on household economy assessment in rural Zimbabwe,* Harare, Zimbabwe.

Scott, James, C. (1998) *Seeing Like a State- How Certain Schemes to Improve the Human Condition Have Failed,* New Haven and London: Yale University Press, pp. 26-30.

Seers, D. (1969) *The meaning of development. Revista Brasileira de Economía,* 24(3), 29-50.

Sen, A. (1999) An ordinal approach to measurement, *Econometria* 46, pp 437-446.

Seidman, A. & Ohiorhenuan, K. (2002) *Twenty first century Africa: Towards a new vision of sustainable development,* Africa world Press, New Jersey.

SESRTCIC Report. (2007) *Poverty in Sub-Saharan Africa,* The situation in the OIC member countries, February 2007.

Sharpley, R. (2015) *Tourism: A vehicle for development.* In R. Sharpley & D. J. Telfer (Eds.), Tourism and Development Concepts and Issues (pp. 3–30). Bristol: Channel View Publications.

Slater, R. & Farrington, J. (2010) Appropriate, Achievable, Acceptable: A practical tool for good targeting. *ODI Social Protection Tool sheet,* ODI, London.

Subbaro, K. (1997) Public works programmes as an anti-poverty programme, An overview of cross-country experience, *American Journal of agric economics,* Vol 1(79):678-679, May 1998.

Subbaro, K., Carlo, D. N., Andrews, C., & Claudia, R. A. (2013) *Public works as safety net,* The World Bank, Washington DC.

Surender, R. (2010) Social Assistance and Dependency in South Africa: An Analysis of Attitudes to Paid Work and Social Grants. *Journal of Social Policy* 39(2): 203-221.

Tekhu, T. and Asefa, S. (1997) Factors affecting employment in labour-intensive public work schemes in rural Botswana, *Economic development and culture change*, 46 (1): 175-186.

Thomas, A. (20000 *Meaning and views of development.* In T. Allen, & A. Thomas (Eds.), Poverty and Development into the 21st Century (pp. 23-48), Oxford University Press, Oxford.

United Nations Development Programme UNDP. (1998) *Human Development Report 1998* New York Oxford University Press.

United Nations Development Programme. (1995) *Human Development Report 1995*, Oxford University Press, New York.

United Nations Development Programme. (2010) *Human Development Report 2010*, Oxford University Press, New York.

URT. (2000) *Poverty Eradication Strategy Paper*, Government Printer, Dar es salaam, Tanzania.

URT. (20050 *The Economic Survey 2004*, Dar-es-salaam, Tanzania.

Valentine, R. T. (1990) *Drought, transfer entitlements, and income distribution: The Botswana experience*, Mimeo, Gaborone.

Wilcock, C. (2009) *Leveraging public works to maximise economic development*, Lukhali projects, Queens Town.

World Bank. (1986) *In transportation development operations policy staff (Ed) The study of the substitution of labour and equipment in civil construction* (SOL) (A research and completion report).

World Bank. (1990) *World development report*, The World Bank, Washington DC.

World Bank. (1997) *Development in practice: Taking actions to reduce poverty in sub-Saharan Africa*, World Bank Publication, Washington DC.

World Bank. (2006) *World development indicators*, The World Bank, Washington D.C.

Wray, C. R. (2009) The social and economic importance of full employment, *Working Paper No*, USA, Kansas City, The Levy Economics Institute of Bard College, University of Missouri.

Printed in the United States
By Bookmasters